CITRUS

RECIPES THAT CELEBRATE
THE SOUR AND THE SWEET

CATHERINE PHIPPS

Photography by Mowie Kay

quadrille

Publishing Director: Sarah Lavelle
Creative Director: Helen Lewis
Senior Designer: Nicola Ellis
Photographer: Mowie Kay
Food Stylist: Marina Filippelli
Prop Stylist: Iris Bromet
Copy Editor: Sally Somers
Production: Tom Moore and Vincent Smith

First published in 2017 by Quadrille Publishing,
Pentagon House, 52–54 Southwark Street,
London SE1 1UN
www.quadrille.co.uk

Quadrille is an imprint of Hardie Grant
www.hardiegrant.com.au

Cataloguing in Publication Data: a catalogue record
for this book is available from the British Library.

ISBN: 978 184949 900 2

contents

For Adam and Lilly

Introduction

Writing about citrus fruits these last months has been a joyous experience.
I can, along with other food writers who reside in the chilly north, live
vicariously through the ingredients I use. I pick up an Italian lemon and
have a strong sense of place – terraced hillsides, a glimpse of Capri blue
sea in the distance, a light breeze made dense by the scent of blossom. It is
romantic and evocative, and just holding and smelling a lemon can bring
that warmth into the most dreary of winter days.

I have been lucky enough to (briefly) live in a place where I could daily pick
limes, sour oranges and grapefruits from the trees. Even now I can regularly
visit my parents in Greece, where the pervasive scent of citrus is forever
entwined with that of the dusty, resinous mountain herbs. However, when I
take time to think about citrus and everything I associate with them,
I realize my overriding memories are rooted in the domestic. I remember
the moment I walked into the kitchen and caught my (then five-year-
old) son studiously zesting one of my best Amalfi lemons, "for the smell,
mummy!". I think about the scent of the kitchen on baking or preserving
days – drizzle cakes warm with a mandarin syrup and shelves lined
with jars of curd and marmalade. A chicken roasting in the oven, its
overwhelming savouriness lifted by a sharp, sweet hit of lemon. The rum
punches during the rained-off summer party, when sour orange juice, stored
from winter, is mixed with sherbety lime. And most recently, the thumbnail
absentmindedly scraping away at the skin of a bergamot or mandarin, also
to release the smell.

I think further back, all the way to my childhood, and realize how the romance of citrus is wrapped up in nostalgia – and the seasons – and that this informs the things I make year on year. And whilst I associate summer with lemons – lemon and elderflower cordial, lemonade, mousses decorated with borage leaves, clean-tasting ice creams – the winter months that fall either side of Christmas are about orange-hued fruits. There is the memory of the satsuma in the Christmas stocking (desiccating peel left on the bedside table, well into January; an instant pot pourri), a small table laden with citrus-flavoured Turkish delight and marzipan sitting alongside Medjool dates, sugared almonds and nuts ready for cracking, and mandarins in the Christmas trifle. These days I also look forward to the leafy citrus displays that appear from November, ready to be transformed into cakes, puddings and liqueurs. I will think about starting Christmas dinner with a palate-awakening puntarelle and orange salad, and make gallons of bergamot- or mandarin-cello. In January, I wait for the first Seville and blood oranges to come into season, for annual marmalade and curd making. And when the late winter palate becomes jaded from all the rich comfort food, and I mourn the loss of bergamots, sour oranges and mandarins, I ease myself into spring by using an abundance of sweet oranges, limes and lemons in salads, soups and casseroles.

I love all of the individual flavours and aromas of citrus, and the fact that I can use them in a wide range of international dishes. Their progression, historically, from East to West means that few cuisines are forced to do without them. And whilst we do make certain associations – lemons mainly with the Mediterranean countries of Europe, the Middle East and Africa, limes belonging to the tropics – it is of course more complicated than that. Every country has made them their own, regardless of climate, presumably as their thick skins and waxy (often now waxed) zest have made them very transportable, as has their keeping ability once preserved. For evidence of this, look no further than the British with our enduring obsession with marmalades, lemonades and citrus desserts such as Sussex Pond Pudding.

Explore the most popular dishes of any particular citrus fruit and you will realize how essential they are to a variety of cuisines we love, and hopefully do not take for granted. For example, the lime. In the UK, limes were once a rarity, found only in processed products, hardly ever found fresh. Now they are everywhere and used as widely as lemons: we zest and juice them into desserts, such as a tart Key lime pie, and we add them along with lemongrass and fragrant kaffir lime leaves to dishes from the Far East. We add their juice to salsas and guacamoles, use them to "cook" fish for ceviche, add them dried to Middle Eastern dishes, pickle them (think sweet/sour in the Americas, searingly hot in India), use them as the basis of the best rum punches, mojitos, caipirinhas. They can also be used in dishes in which lemons are traditional – in fact, in certain areas where nomenclature is ignored, they are used interchangeably anyway.

Lemons, oranges and grapefruit are similarly versatile, and it is probably only a matter of time before yuzu (and who knows what will come next) are as widely available and as ubiquitous. This does not dismay me; on the contrary, I am still eager to explore the possibilities. I have found while researching this book – when I have revisited old favourites as well as experimenting with others – how well citrus fruits can be combined with one another, and how a process used in one particular cuisine, using a particular citrus fruit, can be applied to another. Perhaps the best example of this is yuzukosho, the hot/sour/salty Japanese condiment. It was a truly exciting day when I discovered how well the same method worked with mandarins, lemons and limes.

Above all, I prize citrus for their usefulness. They are simply the most helpful ingredients you can have in your kitchen. Putting aside their own complexity of flavours, they are completely transformative. They enhance savoury qualities of some ingredients and bring out the sweetness and flavours of others. They make ingredients sing, individually and in unison. They can simultaneously add depth and lightness, lifting the flattest of dishes. Citric acid can stop ingredients from turning black and brown. They are preservative and have setting qualities. They can "cook" and tenderize fish and meat. They even help milk become buttermilk, cheese and yogurt. They are also very good for you: not only are they packed full of antioxidants and vitamin C, citrus fruits are credited with helping with everything from hypertension to depression. They are simply miraculous.

Types of Citrus

These pages focus mainly on the citrus fruits that are available to most of us and which, consequently, I have been able to use in recipes – there are of course many, many more with which we are unfamiliar, as hybridization of citrus is and always has been such a popular pastime.

Lemons

Lemons are truly the workhorse in my kitchen, probably the most used ingredient after salt. I cannot imagine life without them. They wheedle their way into everything – if they aren't being used as a dominant flavour, they are acidulating water to stop other ingredients going black or brown, sliced as garnishes in drinks and, most of all, they are used as seasoning alongside salt and pepper. If a dish seems muddy, flat, with indistinct flavours that are not quite gelling, the chances are a squeeze of lemon will sort it out. We do not think of lemons as being seasonal, as they are available all year round – and there is nothing wrong with using a Eureka lemon when nothing better is to hand; it will still have good flavour, acidity and a fragrant zest. However, Italian lemons – in particular those from Amalfi – are worth seeking out when they are in season. These are generally larger with an irregular beauty – they will be knobblier, a pale, indistinct yellow compared to the Eureka, often with the odd bit of mottling or pocking. However, they are sweet and intensely fragrant in comparison.

Meyer lemons are a cross between a lemon and mandarin. They are sweeter than regular lemons, with a very floral-smelling skin which is something between a lemon and orange. Their flesh is more palatable straight and they can be used in the same way as regular lemons, perhaps where you might want less tartness, as they are less acidic.

Sweet lemons are sometimes called sweet limes, as they are found in the Middle East where they aren't big on nomenclature. We can get them in the West at the beginning of the year into early spring. I have made marmalade with them but I don't generally use them in my cooking. They are the same shape and size as a Meyer lemon, but you can tell them apart as their scent is very close to that of a bergamot. In fact, the French do call them bergamot which gets confusing, as they are not the same as the highly perfumed Italian bergamot (see page 12). The zest is extremely fragrant and can be used in anything where you might want to use bergamot, but the juice is much harder to define. If you take a sip after you have just squeezed a sweet lemon, you will be disappointed – the flavour is sweet, watery and insipid, a pale imitation of an orange. Leave it to sit for just a minute or two and it changes beyond all recognition. The juice takes on a bitterness, but with a hint of floral bergamot and a rich, buttery quality in the aftertaste. It's unusual. The longer you leave it (I'm talking minutes, no longer) the more intense this flavour becomes. The Persians juice sweet lemons for immediate consumption or eat the flesh, but only as a cold remedy.

Limes

Limes are so ubiquitous in the UK now that it's strange to think how recent an occurrence this is. This was something I only realized when thinking back to the ways we used citrus when I was growing up. Limes just weren't available outside specialist or ethnic shops. It wasn't until the 1990s that they became commonplace – partly because of all those lime-based cocktails that became so popular (and don't forget of course bottled beers such as Sol which were always sold with a wedge of lime in the top), as well as a growing national obsession with Thai food. The limes available to us are a mixed bag. The most common is the Persian lime – the larger, glossy green sort. These are best defined as good "team players" – they have that very acidic, sherbety flavour, but this often becomes less distinct wherever it is expected to stand alone. Strangely, their flavour does come out much more when being used to accentuate other fruits. For a really good lime flavour look to the **Key or West Indian lime**, which is smaller, more likely to turn yellow when ripe, and has a much more complex flavour and aroma – it is somehow much more floral with spicy notes. Finally, there is also the **kaffir lime**. These are not often available as fruits – they tend to be small, hard and bumpy with very little juice, so are really used for their very fragrant zest – but the real joy in kaffir limes is their sweetly scented leaves which are synonymous with Thai food. For a long time it was extremely difficult to get these leaves fresh – really the only way to use them – but now they are increasingly available in the supermarkets. You can of course use regular lime leaves in cooking too; they are still very fragrant, but not as powerful as kaffir lime, and useful for adding subtle hints of citrus.

Oranges

The orange was my least favourite fruit growing up, for various reasons – I couldn't bear the sticky mess that always resulted from trying to peel and segment them, I didn't like the membrane, and they were just too reminiscent of the horrible UHT cartons of concentrated juice that were available at the time. I didn't see any value in them whatsoever; now I love them in all their variety.

Sour or bitter oranges are without doubt the best and most useful oranges for me in the kitchen. The most common is the Spanish **Seville orange**, although the Italians tend to prefer the chinotto. These are highly perfumed compared to sweeter oranges, with floral, quite intoxicating aromas that are used in a wide range of spirits and liqueurs. Their flowers are also used to make orange blossom water. Sevilles are primarily associated with marmalade, but it is a crime to limit them thus – I use them in place of limes in all sorts of dishes; they are also essential for a proper duck à l'orange, and for the best rum punch. In the UK we get the Seville variety in late winter (the first ones appear in January and have gone by March) and, frustratingly, they are available all year round in tropical parts, but just haven't found their way here yet.

Blood oranges – or blush oranges as they are sometimes called (attempts at sanitization?) – fall somewhere between a sweet and a sour orange. They have a very distinctive flavour, reminiscent of tart summer berries (more wineberry than raspberry) or rhubarb, and a flesh that can be anywhere between a bright orange to black, by way of a rich claret. The depth of colour is dependent on cool night temperatures, which is why the colour varies so much – my first Sicilian batch this year were orange with a few red flecks, and a few weeks later they were almost black. Sadly, the colour of the skin, which also varies from orange to claret, is no indication of the colour within.

Sweet oranges come in a huge variety, and it often feels like a luck of the draw when buying them. Some are just too sweet and insipid to be interesting; others, such as various types of navel oranges, get the sweet/sour balance just right and have a floral complexity on a par with grapefruit. There are textural differences too: certain oranges, such as the Valencian, are much better juiced, as their coarse vesicles and thick membranes make them less pleasant to eat as is.

I have underrated oranges for years – now, as long as they have an element of tartness about them, I use them in all kinds of things, especially savoury salads and roasted with vegetables.

Mandarins and their relatives

These include most of the smaller orange-fleshed fruits such as **tangerines**, **clementines** and **satsumas**. Most of these commercially produced fruits can be used interchangeably if all you are after is sweet, juicy, easy-to-peel orange. However, what I call a "real" mandarin or tangerine is something quite different. The juice will be just the right balance between sweet and tart, but what really sets them apart is the zest. Mandarins are highly fragrant – the first hit is so sweet it is almost reminiscent of an artificially flavoured candy (think Jelly Belly), but this gives way to floral, herby notes (in proper tangerines this is earthier) that are elusive and utterly beguiling. For me, these are the Holy Grail of the citrus world – I spend half the winter looking for them and, when I finally find a supply, frantically buy up as many as I can for preserving purposes, just so I can get a year-round fix. My favourite citrus.

Bergamot Orange

Anyone who has ever drunk Earl Grey tea will be familiar with the scent of **bergamots**. The fruits are deep green, fading to yellow as they ripen; they are somewhere between the size of a large lemon and a grapefruit, with a juice that is quite sour – it is very important not to over-squeeze, as the juice will quickly become bitter if you do so. The fragrance of the zest is exhilarating and almost hypnotic. I find it rich, heavy, with a woody, almost resinous quality. If lemon zest is a light and sweetly floral rambling rose, bergamot is the musky tuber. Its real value, as perfumers throughout the ages have appreciated, is the feeling the scent evokes: I can quite understand how it has mood-lifting attributes. The flavour is subtle in comparison. I find the juice too sour on its own, but it pairs brilliantly with lemons and oranges. It also makes a superb liqueur, or bergamot-cello, which can be added to all manner of cocktails. The season in the northern hemisphere usually runs from October through to very early March.

Grapefruits, Pomelos, Ugli Fruit

Grapefruits are a cross between a pomelo and a sweet orange, which is strange, as both are sweeter – the flesh of a grapefruit is sweet giving way to bitter, and can leave a lingering, fizzy numbness on the palate. It is intensely refreshing and highly perfumed. Over time, the original yellow grapefruit has lost popularity thanks to the sweeter pink and ruby varieties, and commercial juice of all three often goes through a process of "debittering". This is a shame – not just because it makes the juice less healthy (it also removes an antioxidant) but because we lose complexity of flavour along with those bitter notes. For this reason, I never buy grapefruit juice – the extra bitterness of freshly squeezed also pairs much better with sweeter citruses such as mandarin.

Pomelos look like oversized, slightly misshapen grapefruits, but this is deceptive – there is so much pith that the amount of flesh is generally the same. You can use them interchangeably with grapefruit; they are just as refreshing, if slightly sweeter.

Ugli fruit are rarer than pomelos and are a type of tangelo, thought to be a cross between a grapefruit or pomelo, with orange, tangerine or mandarin. The grapefruit and tangerine flavours are there, but much sweeter and nowhere near as pronounced – I think mixing the juice and zest of individual fruits gives a better flavour. A good job really, as they are not easy to come by.

Yuzu

It seems like in a few short years, **yuzu** has become the darling of every chef with any pretensions of being cutting-edge. Does the flavour live up to the hype? I'd give a cautious yes to this. The zest in particular is wonderful – a complex mixture of mandarin, lemon and grapefruit (which, incidentally, can be mixed together to approximate yuzu's flavour). Despite their popularity, actual fruits are still very hard to come by, but juice is available just about everywhere now, as is the zest, preserved in various ways. I have tried many of these, and what really shines is a powdered zest which is extremely versatile. I stir and whisk it into all kinds of things. It is also very good sprinkled over food – use it on savoury dishes in the same way you would use sumac.

Kumquats and Limequats

I'm afraid I do not see a great deal of value in **kumquats**. Their skin is supposed to be sweet and they are one of the few citrus fruits you should be able to eat whole, but I have never enjoyed them thus; I think their flavour works only with copious amounts of sugar, so will usually candy them. **Limequats**, on the other hand, are revelatory. As you would expect, they have an intense lime flavour, but they are somehow lighter, fresher-tasting, and these

I can eat whole. They are mouth-puckering and sherbety on impact, but this gives way to sweetness. I use them in desserts, as garnish, and will also dry and candy them whole.

Finger Limes

These are an Antipodean oddity – green-tinged purple torpedoes jam-packed with distinct vesicles that separate easily for scattering. Each vesicle gives a short, sharp pop of juicy, concentrated lime flavour – it is no wonder they are referred to as "lime caviar". I don't include any recipes using these fruits in particular as, again, they are extremely difficult to come by in the northern hemisphere, but if you do ever manage to acquire some, use them liberally as a garnish on raw or ceviched seafood or fish, salads, desserts and, possibly best of all, in drinks.

Citrus Notes

It is possible to get citrus flavour into your food without recourse to the fruit itself. Herbs such as lemon verbena, lemon balm, lemongrass and lemon myrtle share similar flavour compounds and are variations on a theme – they are all very clean- and fresh-tasting, which makes them good for infusions, especially for creamy desserts and teas. Sorrel does have a pronounced lemony flavour, but with earthier undertones – like lemony Swiss chard or spinach. Finally, spices such as sumac provide a sour hit similar to lemon zest.

Some Citrus Know-how

First of all, it is important to know whether the citrus fruit you are using has been waxed or not. It is not always obvious, so if in doubt, wash the fruit in hot water, lightly rubbing the skin as you do so to remove the wax but so as not to release oil. This is especially important if you are using the zest. Unwaxed fruits are preferable, but they do not store as well as the waxed sort, so these I will always store in the refrigerator.

Believe it or not, there is a right and a wrong way to zest, juice and cut up citrus fruit. In fact, a few years ago I found out that I had been juicing limes wrongly and once I realized what I was doing wrong, it made all the difference to the flavour.

How to Zest

There are several ways to remove zest from a fruit. For a fine grating, you should use a microplane or similar – the rasps will be very fine. Use a very light touch to make sure you are only removing zest and not pith.

For julienned strips of zest, there are two methods. You can use a zester, which ploughs across the skin, leaving ridges of zest behind. So as not to waste this zest I will either use the squeezed carcasses for a simple sugar syrup (see page 215), or go lightly over the whole fruit with a microplane to get a fine grating of everything that was left behind. Alternatively, pare off pieces of zest with a sharp knife or swivel peeler – you will then need to scrape off any white pith, before leaving whole or slicing into julienned strips. This works with the majority of citrus; if you are dealing with very soft, bumpy, thin-skinned fruits (such as some of the smaller orange-skinned fruits), it is better to scrape off the pith from the inside of the peeled skin instead, as it is virtually impossible to pare the zest off from the outside.

How to Juice

The main rule here is don't over-squeeze. If your fruits are very hard and unyielding to the touch, it helps to roll them back and forth on your work surface before cutting them open for juicing. Then, using either a citrus juicer or wooden reamer, squeeze and turn lightly to release the juice. Make sure you don't go in too deep, as you will disturb the white membranes which will release bitter compounds and affect the flavour of the juice (this is the mistake I used to make with limes). I find a reamer easier to use – the main disadvantage is pips, but you can juice over a sieve to collect them if necessary. Of course, for large quantities an electric juicer does help – these should have two sizes to accommodate everything from a lime to a grapefruit.

How to Cut

For thin slices, two pieces of equipment are invaluable: first of all, you need a decent knife. No chef will agree with me on this, but I prefer either a very sharp ceramic knife, or a small serrated knife that will cut through anything with a good degree of precision. Do not use a posh carbon-steel knife as lemon will blacken the blade. I also use a mandoline, but please treat this with caution!

Unless I specify that the skin should be left on, all the recipes in this book require you to prepare citrus so that the skin and at the very least the outer membrane is cut away. The way to do this is to top and tail the citrus and sit it firmly on your chopping board. Then cut from top to bottom, following the contour of the fruit, making sure you are cutting away the pith and outer membrane as you go. When you have cut all the way around, trim off any other bits of white pith you can see. You can then slice or dice the fruit as it is, flicking out pips as you go. For membrane-less segments (often called supremes), take the fruit in one hand and cut along one side of each segment – you can then either cut down the other side to release the segment or you can carefully scrape the flesh in one movement from the centre to the edge – this will ensure you remove every bit of flesh from that side. You should always do this over a bowl to catch any juice, and I always squeeze out the discarded peel and membranes too.

Citrus Economy and Savoury Preserves

If you want to use your citrus fruit to the full, as well as extend the shelf life of some of those with a shorter season, this might well be the chapter you find of most use. You can apply many of the methods here to almost all kinds of citrus, but they are particularly good for capturing the essence of those whose annual visit is fleeting: Seville and blood oranges, proper aromatic mandarins and bergamots. I look forward to the appearance of these fruits every year – I used to hoard them, panic-buying the last sorry-looking specimens, but now I buy them as soon as they are available and make things that I can store for future use, safe in the knowledge that I've done everything possible to preserve flavour. Some recipes you will find in the Sweet Preserves and Sweets chapter, but here you will find everything you need to instantly transform and enhance numerous savoury dishes.

I am a firm believer in keeping to hand all kinds of condiments. This is partly because even though I insist on making pretty much everything from first principles, at heart I am quite a lazy cook. Condiments are a boon to anyone of a similar bent as they can add flavour to simple dishes during the cooking process or at the table. The latter is particularly useful if you are feeding children who might not appreciate the same flavours you do. I find condiments are a means for stumbling across interesting flavour combinations. For me, this usually happens at lunchtime when I have leftovers in the refrigerator – it is how I discovered that any kind of sweet, creamy curd cheese is superb not just with citrus oil and preserved lemons, but with all the "koshos" too, that leftover roast lamb is incredible when put in a sandwich with preserved blood orange, finely chopped dates, mint and chilli, and that some leftover chowder or fish pie is given a whole new complexity by having some finely chopped sweet lime pickle stirred through it.

The traditional methods of preserving citrus generally require time and patience – you will have to delay gratification for weeks if not months. However, there are a few shortcut recipes in this chapter that I think actually improve on the originals. They are quick, easy and provide the freshest of flavours.

Drying

What to Dry?

It is possible to dry everything from finely microplaned zest to whole fruit, which can be used in rubs, sugars, salts and seasonings, for perfuming stews, casseroles and rice dishes, or in teas and tisanes.

Zest

The most versatile type of dried citrus is the zest. It is best to peel it away from the skin in wide strips and scrape off any remaining pith. This is what I use to add a gentle perfume and flavour to dishes such as a classic French fish soup or a beef casserole.

Microplaned zest dries very quickly and is best finely ground to a powder in a pestle and mortar, then added either right at the beginning of a dish, by way of a rub, or right at the end, as a seasoning, in the same way you might use pepper, sumac, or even fennel pollen.

Dried Peel

This includes the pith as well as the zest. You can cut this into strips in the same way you would when making marmalade, or you can leave it in big pieces. The former is particularly good in rice – the only issue is that before using, you really need to blanch it two or three times so it doesn't make your dish too bitter. Larger pieces can be broken up and added to your own blends of teas, or used during barbecuing and smoking – adding dried citrus will scent the smoke that envelops your food, adding subtle aroma and a hint of flavour.

Slices of Citrus

Using cross-section slices is perhaps the most decorative way of drying citrus – these look beautiful left whole and added to hot drinks. Cut them as thinly as you can, preferably with a mandoline. You can also use dried slices to make citrus powder or "dust" (see page 18).

Whole Citrus

You can buy dried limes, or "loomi", in many Middle Eastern shops, and they add distinctive, sherbety sour and earthy flavours to all kinds of dishes. They come in two strengths – the light ochre-coloured ones are milder, whilst the black ones have had a much longer drying time and taste more pungent. It is quite a simple process to make these at home (see page 18), and you can also experiment with other types of citrus (smaller varieties are best). The whole fruit are best pierced and can be used to flavour stews or casseroles, to make tea (this is a bit of an acquired taste), or even ground to a fine powder.

How to Dry

This is a very simple process; you'll already be familiar with it if you've ever come across abandoned peel that has desiccated naturally. If you are in a hurry, simply put your peel/zest or slices on a wire rack and toast in the oven (on its lowest setting, if above 100°C/200°F, with the door slightly ajar) for anything between 30 minutes and 3 hours, depending on what you are drying, until they are parchment-dry. The slices will obviously take longer than the peel, as they contain much more water, but try to avoid letting them brown too much as you don't want them to taste burnt – the original colour should be preserved as much as possible. If you have space and time, arrange on a rack again and leave somewhere warm and dry, for example in an airing cupboard, near a radiator or on a sunny windowsill. The slices will probably take 2–3 days to dry out completely. The best way to store dried citrus is in an airtight container, somewhere cool and dark. As picturesque as strings of citrus slices look, they will not keep their flavour or colour in the same way.

The method for drying whole fruit is slightly more involved. You have probably inadvertently made them yourself at some point (ever left a lime to languish in the fruit bowl until it is rock solid? I have...) and it is true that you can make them by leaving them somewhere dry and sunny. However, to stop them going mouldy before they have completely dried out, it is better to boil them in salted water (add slightly more salt than you would when cooking pasta) for 15 minutes. Then drain, dry thoroughly and leave on a wire rack somewhere sunny, or speed up the process by putting them in a low oven and leaving them until they are light and hollow-sounding when tapped; it is up to you how dark you want them. I have dried limequats and my favourite winter mandarins in this way too.

Powdered Citrus or "Dust"

Any kind of citrus fruit – and indeed any part of the citrus – can be ground into powder. I make quite small amounts at a time and mix and match at will, which ensures that the flavours stay fresh. Very simply, dry slices of citrus as described above. When completely dry (no tackiness at all), allow to cool then grind to a powder in a small food processor with a large pinch each of sugar and salt.

Citrus Salts and Rubs

You can add dried citrus to salt, sugar and other aromatics to make salts, rubs and decorative dusts for sweet desserts and bakes. It is up to you whether you use strips of dried zest or slices for this (I don't recommend using peel) – it depends on how dominant and zesty you want your finished salt or rub to be.

The variety of rubs you can make is limited only by the contents of your spice cupboard and your imagination. I think lime works particularly well with all kinds of chilli – try these combinations, making sure you add a teaspoon of salt and some black peppercorns to the mix.

- Lime/chipotle/oregano/coriander seed/cinnamon

- Lime (or sour orange)/Scotch bonnet/thyme/allspice/cinnamon/mace/powdered garlic

- Lime or lemon/Kashmiri chilli/cayenne/turmeric/coriander seed/mustard seed

Other favourite combinations include:
- Sour orange/Szechuan peppercorns/coriander seed/cayenne
- Lemon/cardamom/coriander seed/ground ginger
- Lemon or orange/bay/allspice
- Grapefruit and/or lemon/fennel seeds/black pepper
- Mandarin or tangerine/smoked sweet paprika/thyme

Freezing Citrus

Citrus freezes remarkably well, depending on what you want to use the citrus fruit for. I always freeze as much Seville orange juice as I can every February, as I love using it in rum punches, which I want to drink more in the summer than winter.

Juice: Freeze in ice-cube trays, small tubs or bags in measured quantities so you know exactly what you've got.

Zest: Open freeze zest, either microplaned or in strips, then when it is solid, decant into small tubs or bags. You can also freeze zest in ice-cube trays covered in oil or citrus juice. Use the citrus-infused oil to start off the frying/sautéeing process in a meal, or for making a salad dressing. Use the zest and juice cubes for anything you need both in.

Wedges: All of the smaller citrus fruits work especially well here for adding to drinks – I use small lemons, limes, blood oranges and mandarins. Open-freeze on a tray then transfer to a freezer bag or container.

Slices: Again, these are good added to drinks where it's not essential for them to keep their form. Open-freeze on a tray then transfer to a freezer bag or container.

Whole: Citrus fruits don't keep their shape well after freezing, but this is an ideal way to keep them fresh if you want to use them for marmalade or jelly. So, if you don't have time to make Seville marmalade in February, all is not lost – you can store them in freezer bags until you need them.

How to Make Citrus Oil

This is best done in small amounts, as its freshness will disintegrate over time. I only make around 200ml/about ¾ cup at once. I always use pared pieces of zest rather than a fine microplane and I pretty much always use olive oil – if a fairly mild-flavoured one.

As usual, there is a long method and a short method. You can put the zest (pared into strips is best) of the citrus of your choice in a sterilized jar and cover with oil, then leave somewhere sunny and warm to infuse for a couple of weeks. Then strain into a sterilized bottle and keep in the refrigerator. Or you can put the zest in a saucepan with the oil, simmer for 5 minutes, then for a fairly light, clean-looking oil, remove the pared zest and decant the oil to a bottle, or for a stronger infusion, leave to cool, then strain and decant.

You can of course add other flavours to these oils, but I do find they are more versatile on their own. Use them to drizzle over grilled fish or chicken, and as a base for salad dressings or marinades in place of regular oil.

Preserved Lemons
(and other citrus)

I imagine most of us are familiar with preserved lemons – the sort we associate with Morocco, although it isn't a process exclusive to North Africa; I have found similar all over Asia and the Americas too. The usual method is to leave whole or almost quartered lemons to steep in heavily salted water or lemon juice. This is extremely simple to do – it just requires a certain amount of patience. Simply top and tail the lemons (or limes, or Seville oranges – you need a fairly acidic fruit for this), then cut a deep cross through each one, almost – but not quite – to the base. Stuff each lemon with sea salt (around 2 teaspoons in each), then pack tightly into a sterilized preserving jar. Weigh the fruit down if possible – I find scalded muslin wrapped around traditional weights or a well-scrubbed tin works – then leave for a couple of days. Remove the weights, muddle the lemons a bit with a wooden spoon to try to release more juice (some will already have collected in the base of the jar), then top with freshly squeezed lemon juice until the lemons are completely covered. Seal, then leave to mature for at least 4 weeks. They can then be kept for over a year in the refrigerator once you have opened them.

Variations
You can add aromatics to the lemons when you add the lemon juice. Black peppercorns, cardamom and bay leaves are all good.

Other Citrus
You can apply the same method to limes and Seville oranges. In fact, researching this solved a long-standing conundrum for me. I had always wondered what the "lime pickles" in *Little Women* were: you know the ones – used as currency amongst Amy March's schoolfriends and the source of a great humiliation when she is forced to throw them, two at a time, out of the classroom window. These, I think, are best cut through into quarters. Add 2 tsp salt per lime and leave to stand in the same way, then cover with lime juice, adding any aromatics. I like mace blades and allspice berries or cinnamon sticks and star anise, perhaps with a few dried chilli (red pepper) flakes sprinkled in. I have made them plain and tried to imagine a group of teenage girls wanting to chew on them, and can almost see it – they are salty, sherbety and mouth-puckering, and will make your mouth go numb in the same way as a bag of Haribo sours. So yes, strangely addictive.

Cheat's Preserved Lemons
(or Limes, or Oranges …)

4 lemons (or any other type of citrus, see introduction, right)

1 tsp sea salt

And here is the one recipe in this chapter I absolutely could not do without. It is an instant version of preserved lemons I discovered in Anna Hansen's *The Modern Pantry* cookbook and it's a brilliant way of getting that potent, salty burst of citrus into dishes when you haven't homemade preserved lemons to hand or you don't want to shell out for the generally substandard and ridiculously expensive bought variety. And actually, I find this version brighter and more versatile – the juice is salty, but not overly so, and has an intense, citrusy flavour which makes it ideal in dressings or just drizzled over some fish or chicken to brighten it up. I have made this with Seville oranges, blood oranges, mandarins (tricky because of the thin mandarin skin but do-able; just accept that you need to scrape pith from the inside, rather than pare zest from the outside), limes and grapefruit. All wonderful. Citrus preserved this way will keep indefinitely in the refrigerator, but will gradually lose its vibrancy of colour. To preserve it for longer, you can freeze it.

Pare the zest from the lemons in large slices, preferably with a swivel peeler, then trim off any excess white pith. Put in a small saucepan, squeeze the pared lemons and add the juice to the pan along with the sea salt. Bring to the boil, then turn down the heat and simmer for around 10 minutes or until the zest is tender.

Allow to cool and keep in a sterilized jar in the refrigerator until needed. It will keep for months, but can be used immediately.

Yuzukosho and other koshos

This is a Japanese condiment made from very finely chopped yuzu zest and chilli. It's hot, salty, very sour but with floral notes coming through that really lift it. As it is very difficult to buy fresh yuzu, if you want an authentic yuzukosho, you will probably need to buy it ready-made. However, I have found that you can use the same principles and adapt them to other kinds of chilli and citrus, which is what I've done here. If you are lucky enough to find some fresh yuzu, remember that the basic formula is four times the amount of chilli to zest. Then weigh and add 10 per cent of the final weight in salt. This formula can be messed around with as much as you like, depending on the type of chillies you use, with the chilli/zest ratio very adaptable. However, the salt must always be 10 per cent of the total.

To prepare, simply put everything in a food processor or grind with a pestle and mortar. It tastes good from the start, but try to leave it in the refrigerator to ferment gently for a week and the flavour will be vastly improved. After that, it will keep indefinitely.

Here are a couple of examples of my favourite mixes, making relatively small amounts – a little does go a long way, though.

15g/½oz finely grated lemon zest (from around 4 large lemons)

5g/⅙oz finely grated mandarin zest (from around 4 mandarins)

40g/1½oz medium-hot red chillies, deseeded and finely chopped

6g/¼oz salt

Lemon-mandarin-kosho

When you can get very fragrant mandarins, around February/March time, the flavour of this version can be wonderfully complex and subtle for such a punch-packing condiment.

continued...

20g/¾oz finely grated lime zest

5g/⅒oz Scotch bonnet chilli, deseeded and finely chopped

35g/1¼oz mild-medium-hot red or green chillies, deseeded and finely chopped

6g/¼oz salt

Lime-Scotch bonnet-kosho

Good for adding a hot/sour note to sweet coconut milk dishes. If you want to make this very hot, just increase the amount of Scotch bonnet chilli and reduce the amount of mild – I have included just a small amount for flavour as opposed to heat.

Once you have some kosho stored in the refrigerator, you can use it in any number of ways. I use it in its pure form as a condiment for soup, or spread on grilled meat or fish. You can turn it into a thinner sauce with some lime juice and a pinch of sugar or honey, and it makes an incredible dipping sauce with soy sauce and juice. You can add other aromatics to it such as garlic and ginger. And if you need to offset the sweetness from other ingredients in your dish, add this kosho to an oil-based dressing – for example, try it with the sweetest, height-of-the-season tomatoes.

Lime-Pickled Red Onions

1 large red onion, thinly sliced

100ml/7 tbsp lime juice

1 tsp salt

A few cracked peppercorns

To serve

Freshly chopped herbs, such as coriander (cilantro) or parsley

1 tsp sumac

These are unbelievably quick and easy and keep in the refrigerator for several weeks. I particularly like them with the Marinated Chicken on page 106.

Put the onions in a bowl and pour over freshly boiled water to cover. Leave to stand for 20 seconds, then drain.

In a small bowl, mix the lime juice with the salt. Pour over the onions, add the peppercorns and stir to combine. If serving straight away, leave to stand for at least 30 minutes. Otherwise, transfer to a sterilized jar and store in the refrigerator until needed.

To serve, add the fresh herbs (choose whichever matches the dish you are serving it with) and a sprinkling of sumac.

Sweet Lime Pickle

Makes about 1 x 500ml/2 cup jar

5 limes, plus 150ml/10 tbsp lime juice
75g/generous ¼ cup fine sea salt
200g/1 cup granulated sugar
1 tsp allspice berries
1 tsp black peppercorns
2 cloves

This to me has the perfect balance of sweet/sour. I particularly like it as an accompaniment to grilled fish. For a hot lime pickle you could add chilli to this, but you could also use the recipe for the Lemon Curry on page 128, which is very similar to the traditional lime pickle we Brits like to eat with poppadoms.

Give the limes a good wash under hot water. Dry off, then top and tail quite generously. Slice the limes thinly, then arrange in a single layer over kitchen paper. Sprinkle over half the salt, then cover with more kitchen paper and leave to stand for 5 hours.

Turn over the lime slices (you should see that the salt has dissolved) and cover with the remaining salt, and a layer of kitchen paper. Leave for another few hours or, even better, overnight.

Rinse the lime slices thoroughly to get rid of any excess salt, then put in a saucepan and cover with water. Bring to the boil, turn down and simmer very gently for around 30 minutes until the lime slices are tender but still intact. Drain carefully into a warmed sterilized jar.

While you are simmering the lime slices, make the spiced syrup. Put the sugar, lime juice and spices in a saucepan with 75ml/5 tbsp water. Heat slowly until the sugar has dissolved, then simmer until it has thickened to a syrup. This should take about as long as the lime slices.

Pour the syrup over the lime slices, straining it if you like. Seal and leave for at least 3 weeks before using. After that the lime slices will keep indefinitely in the refrigerator.

Soups

When I work through my list of favourite soups and broths, I am hard pushed to find many that don't include citrus in some form or another. Even comforting, creamy soups benefit from a judicious squeeze of lemon juice to cut through the richness and give a more rounded flavour. Lemon in particular is alchemical – I cannot count the number of times I have made a soup and been disappointed in the flavour, until I've remembered to squeeze in just a few drops. The result is instantaneous – the flavours become distinct, but also meld together perfectly; there is a depth and balance that just wasn't there before. This works so well, it almost feels like cheating. Any of the more sour citrus fruits will work in this way but none is as effective as lemon.

Citrus as a garnish can also change a soup completely. This is where some of the condiments in the previous chapters come into play. Try adding preserved citrus to mellow, creamy lentil- or bean-based soups, beat citrus zest and a touch of juice into ricotta and drop into slightly thickened soups and broths, add any variant of "kosho" in unadulterated form or mixed with oil and finely chopped herbs to give salty, hot and sour notes to sweet roast vegetable or squash soups. All of this is particularly useful when you want to add bursts of strong flavour to individual bowls of soup – whether it's because you have leftovers you want to jazz up a bit, or simply because you have kept soup on the bland side for feeding children who don't appreciate sourness and heat.

Fish Broth with Lime Leaves, Lemongrass and Coconut

Serves 4

For the fish

600g/1lb 5oz firm white fish fillets,
skinned and cut into chunks or slices

Finely grated zest and juice of 2 limes

3 garlic cloves, crushed

½ Scotch bonnet chilli, finely chopped

Sea salt and black pepper

For the paste

4 spring onions (scallions), sliced

3 garlic cloves, roughly chopped

5cm/2-in piece of fresh root ginger,
peeled and roughly chopped

3 lemongrass stalks, whites only,
roughly chopped

½ Scotch bonnet chilli, deseeded
and chopped

½ tsp allspice berries

½ tsp coriander seeds

A small bunch of mint, leaves only

Finely grated zest and juice of 2 limes

For the soup

400ml/generous 1½ cups fish stock

400ml/generous 1½ cups coconut milk

1 tbsp fish sauce or light soy sauce

A sprig of thyme

A few lime leaves, preferably not kaffir

1 aubergine (eggplant), diced

1 red (bell) pepper, sliced into strips

A medium bag of spinach, or callaloo

Cooked rice or noodles, a few basil
leaves, a squeeze of lime juice, to serve

This isn't a Thai broth, although the method and flavours are similar – it is based on my attempt years ago to make a kind of Caribbean version of Thai green curry paste. There is a lot of overlap of ingredients, obviously; the biggest difference is no coriander (cilantro), instead we have the woody thyme we associate with Caribbean food, as well as mint and basil for sweetness. We don't automatically associate lemongrass with the Caribbean, but it is often grown as a cash crop as well as being used in the local bush teas and tisanes.

First marinate the fish. Put in a bowl and season generously with salt and pepper. Mix the lime zest and juice with the garlic and chilli, then dilute with 100ml/7 tbsp water. Pour this over the fish and leave to stand for around 30 minutes.

Meanwhile, make the paste. Put all the ingredients in a small food processor with some salt and pepper, and blend until fairly smooth.

Put the stock, coconut milk and fish sauce or soy in a large saucepan or flameproof casserole. Add the thyme, lime leaves and all but a tablespoon of the paste. Bring to the boil and simmer gently for 2 minutes, then add the aubergine (eggplant) and red (bell) pepper. Simmer until almost tender, around 10 minutes, then add the greens. When they have wilted down, drain the fish, pat it dry and add to the broth. Simmer for a couple of minutes.

Serve over a small amount of rice or noodles, sprinkled with basil leaves and with a squeeze of lime.

Lime and Chicken Tortilla Soup

Serves 4

For the chicken and marinade

2 boneless, skinless chicken
  breasts, butterflied

Finely grated zest and juice of 1 lime

1 tsp each of chipotle chilli powder,
  garlic powder and dried oregano

½ tsp smoked salt

1 tbsp olive oil

For the soup

2 tbsp olive oil

1 red onion, finely diced

2 red (bell) peppers, finely diced

2 celery sticks, finely diced

500g/1lb 2oz very ripe tomatoes

1 head of garlic, broken into cloves

1 chipotle chilli, whole but deseeded

3 tbsp finely chopped coriander
  (cilantro) stems (save leaves
  for garnish)

A large sprig of thyme

1 litre/generous 4 cups chicken stock

200g/generous 1 cup cooked black
  beans (optional)

For the garnishes

1 avocado

Juice of 1 lime

2–3 tbsp olive oil

2–3 corn tortillas, cut into triangles

100ml/7 tbsp soured cream

A few coriander (cilantro) leaves

Grated hard cheese, such as Manchego,
  Gruyère or Cheddar (or see above)

This has quite a lot of elements to it and ends up being a bit of an assembly job towards the end. It's not a true tortilla soup (I don't like soggy tortillas, much better to have them as a crisp garnish), more of a cross between that and *sopa de lima*. You can play around with the garnishes as much as you want. Crumbled feta – which is really a salty version of the Latin American *queso fresco* – would work instead of a hard cheese, as would a traditional guacamole in place of the avocado.

Put the chicken breasts in a bowl. Mix together the marinade ingredients and pour this over the chicken. Leave to marinate for 1 hour. Heat a griddle pan until it is too hot to hold your hand over. Griddle the chicken for 3–4 minutes on each side until just cooked through. Set aside.

Heat the oil for the soup in a large flameproof casserole or saucepan. Add the onion, red (bell) peppers and celery. Sauté on a low heat until translucent and starting to caramelize lightly. This will take at least 10–15 minutes. Meanwhile, put the tomatoes, unpeeled garlic cloves and chilli in a heavy-based frying pan and dry roast for a similar amount of time until the tomatoes are blackening. If the chilli and garlic look done before the tomatoes, fish them out and put to one side. Peel the garlic cloves and put in a food processor with the unpeeled tomatoes and chilli. Blitz until smooth.

Add the coriander (cilantro) stems and thyme sprig to the onion pan and cook for a couple of minutes. Pour in the tomato mixture and simmer for 5 minutes until starting to reduce. Add the chicken stock and continue to simmer for around 15–20 minutes.

For the garnishes, dice the avocado and toss in the lime juice. Heat the oil in a large frying pan and fry the tortilla triangles until crisp and golden brown. Shred the chicken and add it to the soup along with the black beans, if using. Remove the thyme sprig and serve the soup garnished with the tortillas, avocado, soured cream, coriander (cilantro) leaves and cheese.

Chicken, Chard and Giant Couscous Soup

Serves 4

1 tbsp olive oil

1 tbsp butter

2 leeks, cut into thin rounds

2 garlic cloves, finely chopped

Finely grated zest of 1 lemon or lime

A bunch of chard, leaves only, shredded

50g/1¾oz yellow beans, halved

50g/1¾oz runner beans, halved

1 litre/generous 4 cups well-flavoured
chicken stock

200g/7oz cooked giant couscous
(about 60g/2oz uncooked weight)

200g/7oz cooked chicken, torn
into chunks

Sea salt and freshly ground black
pepper

A few shavings of Parmesan, to
serve (optional)

For the harissa dressing

25g/1½ cups fresh parsley leaves

10g/¾ cup fresh mint leaves

10g/¾ cup fresh coriander
(cilantro) leaves

½ tsp ground cardamom

½ tsp ground fennel seed

½ tsp ground coriander

1 garlic clove, crushed

1 green chilli (optional)

1 tbsp preserved lemon or lime
(see page 21 for homemade)

50ml/3½ tbsp olive oil

Juice of ½ lemon or 1 lime

A few fresh lemon verbena
leaves (optional)

This soup started out as a collection of leftovers in my refrigerator – the first time I made it, the cooked chicken had a subtle aroma of bergamot (see Bergamot and Lemon Roast Chicken, page 103). Citrus delicately pervades the soup, but the harissa-style dressing really adds another dimension to the flavour. It's a bit like adding pistou to minestrone.

Heat the olive oil and butter in a large saucepan or flameproof casserole. When the butter has melted, add the leeks with a splash of water and season with salt and pepper. Cover and cook very gently for 10 minutes, checking every so often, until tender and buttery. Add the garlic and cook for a further couple of minutes, trying not to stir too much.

Add the zest, chard leaves and beans, then pour over the stock. Bring to the boil then reduce the heat and simmer for a few minutes until the beans are tender, then add the couscous and chicken. Continue to simmer just to warm through.

While the soup is simmering, make the harissa dressing. Simply put everything in a food processor and blitz until you have a fresh-looking green paste – you may have to thin with a little water if you are finding it recalcitrant. Taste for seasoning and add salt if necessary.

Serve the soup with spoonfuls of the dressing stirred in at the last minute, with a few shavings of Parmesan, if you like.

Orange, Melon and Ginger Gazpacho

Serves 4

½ large orange-fleshed melon, peeled and deseeded (prepared weight around 500g/1lb 2oz)

1 large cucumber, peeled, halved lengthways and deseeded

A small knob of fresh root ginger, peeled

¼ red (bell) pepper, roughly chopped

2 spring onions (scallions), whites only, roughly chopped

Finely grated zest and juice of 1 lime

Juice of 1 orange or 2 mandarins

½ tsp white wine vinegar

Sea salt

To serve

A small bunch of mint, coriander (cilantro) or basil, leaves only

50ml/3½ tbsp olive oil

Lime wedges

This makes a refreshing change from the red tomato version, and is best made at the height of summer, which is about the only time we can get really good melons. You can make this slightly more savoury with a couple of green tomatoes or, even better, tomatillos if you have them.

If you are serving this as soon as you have made it, make sure all your ingredients are very well chilled, and have a few ice cubes to hand to add at the end.

Put all the gazpacho ingredients in a blender with a generous pinch of salt and blitz until smooth, then decant into a refrigerator-friendly container and chill until you are ready to serve. Blitz the herbs with the olive oil and a generous pinch of salt and serve the gazpacho drizzled over with the herb oil, and with lime wedges on the side.

Lamb and Dried Lime Soup

Serves 4

1 tbsp olive oil

2 red onions, fairly finely chopped

500g/1lb 2oz lamb, trimmed of fat
  and cut into 1–2cm/½–¾-in cubes

1 tsp ground turmeric

1 tsp ground coriander

1 tsp ground cumin

1 tsp ground ginger

½ tsp ground cinnamon

¼ tsp ground cardamom

A pinch of ground cloves

4 garlic cloves, finely chopped

50g/1¾oz bunch of coriander (cilantro),
  stems and leaves separated, finely
  chopped

50g/1¾oz bunch of parsley, stems and
  leaves separated, finely chopped

1 tbsp tomato paste

1 litre/generous 4 cups chicken, lamb
  or vegetable stock

50g/¼ cup red lentils, well rinsed

6 dried limes (see page 18)

2 roasted red (bell) peppers, cut or
  pulled into strips

250g/1¾ cups cooked chickpeas
  (garbanzo beans)

A squeeze of lemon juice

Sea salt and freshly ground black
  pepper

This is a soup that incorporates lots of flavours I associate with Middle Eastern food, but it doesn't really conform to any specific dish. It's quite beautiful – a deep ochre colour flecked with fresh green and yellow. You can use the brown or black dried limes in this recipe, and it's up to you whether you crush them up and leave them in to be eaten. I love the sour hit combined with the other ingredients, but it might be a bit much for some. You can use any cut of lamb here, but just make sure you trim it of any excess fat.

Heat the oil in a large flameproof casserole or saucepan. Add the onions and cook on a gentle heat until well softened and lightly golden. Turn up the heat and add the lamb. Sear quickly on all sides, then add all the spices, the garlic, coriander (cilantro) stems and parsley stems and the tomato paste. Stir until you have a rich brown gravy (the lamb will give out some liquid), then season with salt and pepper, pour in the stock and sprinkle in the red lentils.

Pierce the dried limes several times with a fork, then add these to the pan, pushing them under until they sink (they will be buoyant until they take in a little liquid). Bring to the boil, then turn down the heat to low, cover and simmer for around 30 minutes.

Squash the limes against the side of the pan with the back of a wooden spoon to help them release flavour, then add the red (bell) peppers and the chickpeas (garbanzo beans) to the soup. Simmer for another 10 minutes. Stir through the chopped fresh herb leaves and add the lemon juice.

Serve as it is, or with rice or couscous.

Small Plates

There came a point during the writing of this chapter when I realized that it was being completely overrun with variations on the raw fish/citrus combination. I have always loved ceviche, first experienced not in Peru, but in the Grenadines. I stepped off a sailing boat with a freshly caught conch; some American friends headed straight for the quayside market, bought fresh limes, Scotch bonnets and salt, and taught me how to make conch ceviche right there and then. I've been hooked ever since, trying everything from a simple Italian crudo (all you need is slivers of white fish, olive oil and a scant amount of lemon zest and juice) to a Fijian kokoda. Recipes for lightly "cooked" or pickled fish in citrus fruit have obvious commonality, but they are also incredibly diverse. I have focused on my favourite flavour combinations, but you can adapt to any types of citrus and chilli you like – just remember you need a degree of acidity, so lemons, limes, sour oranges, yuzu are good, whereas others such as sweet oranges and mandarins are lovely for flavour but need to be paired with something sharper.

Whilst I love all the dishes in this chapter, the one I am particularly proud of and really must entreat you to try is the Deep-fried Citrus Slices (see page 46). These are addictive – the citrus is firmly centre stage rather than given a supporting role.

Mediterranean-Inspired Mezze

Serves 4

500g/3½ cups cooked chickpeas
(garbanzo beans), the equivalent of
2 x 400g tins (or start with dried, see
introduction), plus 1–2 ladlefuls of
the liquid from the tin/cooking liquid

Juice of 1 lemon

2 garlic cloves, crushed or grated

4 tbsp tahini

Olive oil, for drizzling

1 preserved lemon, skin only (or 2 tbsp
of the quick sort, see page 22)

A sprinkling of sumac or paprika

Sea salt

Preserved Lemon Hummus

**I tried all kinds of preserved citrus with this, and lemon
definitely works best, although I do also like using lime,
with a sprinkling of allspice and cayenne on top, or
orange with a sprinkling of dried mountain herbs.
If you are using dried chickpeas (garbanzo beans),
which are so much better than using tinned, then you
will need to start with about a third of the weight/
volume of cooked. They will need an overnight soak,
a rinse, and then simmering for 1–2 hours, depending
on how old they are.**

Put the drained chickpeas (garbanzo beans) in a blender
with half the lemon juice, the garlic and the tahini and a
little of the reserved liquid. Blitz, pushing down regularly,
adding a little more liquid if necessary. Season with salt
and taste. Add more garlic and lemon juice if you like, and
blitz again. You should end up with a soft consistency, but
it should hold its shape at all times.

To serve, transfer to a bowl and drizzle with olive oil. Cut
the preserved lemon into a fine dice and sprinkle centrally
over the hummus. If using the quick preserved lemon,
drizzle over a little of the liquor too. Sprinkle with a little
sumac, or paprika if you prefer.

400g/14oz large green olives (or a
mixture of green and black)

Pared and julienned zest and juice
of 1 lemon

2 garlic cloves, very thinly sliced

½ tsp dried chilli flakes (red pepper
flakes) or 1 fresh chilli, finely chopped

½ tsp dried rosemary, or several sprigs
of fresh rosemary, roughly chopped

2 tbsp olive oil

Marinated Olives

Rinse the olives of any brine or oil, then mix with all
the remaining ingredients. Leave to stand for at least an
hour before serving, but if you can, do them at least a
day in advance.

continued...

Small plates

continued…

250g/9oz block of halloumi, cut into 16 pieces

1 tbsp ouzo

1 tsp dried oregano

16 lemon leaves (or bay, see introduction)

Olive oil, plus extra to serve

Lemon wedges, to serve

Barbecued Halloumi in Lemon Leaves

It's quite incredible how well the lemon leaves scent the cheese when cooked this way. If you don't have citrus leaves, a good option is to add lemon zest to the ouzo and oregano and wrap the cheese in large, freshly picked bay leaves.

Heat a griddle pan until too hot to hold your hand near, or get a barbecue ready. Toss the halloumi in the ouzo and oregano. Brush the lemon (or bay) leaves lightly with olive oil then wrap each piece of halloumi in a leaf, securing with a toothpick.

Put the halloumi on the griddle or barbecue and cook for 2 minutes on each side until the leaves are starting to burn and the halloumi has softened.

Unwrap, leaving the halloumi on the leaves, and drizzle with a little more olive oil. Serve with the lemon wedges.

2 oranges

50g/scant ⅓ cup fine bulgar wheat

½ red onion, finely chopped

2 medium tomatoes, finely chopped

½ cucumber, finely diced

A large bunch of flat-leaf parsley, roughly chopped

A small bunch of mint, roughly chopped

Sea salt and freshly ground black pepper

For the dressing

Finely grated zest and juice of ½ lemon

2 tbsp olive oil

1 small garlic clove, crushed

A pinch of ground cumin

A pinch of ground cinnamon

A pinch of ground allspice

A pinch of ground cloves

1 tsp honey or pomegranate molasses

Parsley and Orange Tabbouleh

Segment the oranges (see page 15) over a bowl to catch any juice, cut into dice and set aside. Squeeze out the peel and membranes into the juice.

Rinse the bulgar wheat in plenty of cold water. Drain thoroughly and put in a bowl. Add the onion, tomatoes, cucumber, herbs and diced orange, and season with salt.

Add the reserved juice to all the dressing ingredients and season with salt and pepper. Whisk together. Pour this over the salad just before you are about to eat and toss lightly.

continued…

continued...

Zest of 1 lemon, preferably dried

1 tsp smoked sea salt

¼ tsp sweet smoked paprika

¼ tsp hot paprika

200g/1½ cups whole blanched almonds

2 tsp olive oil

A pinch of citric acid (optional, but
    adds an extra hit of sour fizziness)

Lemon and Paprika Spiced Almonds

If using dried lemon zest, mix it with the smoked salt
and both paprikas and blitz in a small food processor
until powdery. If using fresh lemon zest, preheat your
oven to its lowest temperature, finely grate the zest and
spread over a baking tray. Leave in the oven with the door
ajar for around 30 minutes or so until dry. Cool, then
proceed as for dried lemon zest.

Put the almonds in a single layer in a large frying pan.
Toast lightly for a few minutes, stirring or shaking
regularly, until golden brown. Add the olive oil, powdered
zest mixture and citric acid, if using, and stir until the
almonds are coated. Remove from the heat and cool
before serving.

Makes 6 long or 12 short flatbreads

225g/about 1¾ cups spelt flour

A pinch of baking powder

A pinch of dried instant yeast

1 tsp sea salt

1 tsp runny honey

100ml/7 tbsp tepid water

50ml/3½ tbsp olive oil, plus extra
    for brushing

Finely grated zest of 1 lemon

Za'atar and sumac, for sprinkling

Crispbreads for Mezze

**This is quite a versatile recipe – the dough is soft and
pliable without too much bounceback so it is easy to
work. You can cook it until crisp, as I've suggested here,
or cook it for less time for a softer bread. If you want
a softer flatbread, I suggest you roll the dough into
rounds rather than an oblong shape.**

Preheat your oven to 220°C/425°F/Gas Mark 7.

Put the flour in a bowl with the baking powder and yeast.
Mix briefly then add the salt, honey, water and olive
oil. Mix until you have a smooth dough, resisting the
temptation to add extra flour, then turn out onto a work
surface. Knead for a couple of minutes, then return to the
bowl, cover with a damp cloth or plastic wrap and leave
for around 30 minutes.

Divide the dough into 6 or 12 pieces, depending how long
you want them to be, then roll each into a lozenge shape.
Lay out over 2–3 baking trays, then prick all over with a
fork, brush with oil and sprinkle with the lemon zest and
some za'atar and sumac.

Bake for 10–12 minutes until crisp and turning a rich
ochre. Dust with a little more za'atar and sumac if you like.

Black Bean Cakes with Lime and Mango Salsa

Serves 4

For the bean cakes

1 tbsp olive oil, plus extra for brushing

A small bunch of spring onions (scallions), finely sliced (include some of the greens)

½ red (bell) pepper, finely diced

2 garlic cloves, finely chopped

1 tsp ground cumin

½ tsp ground coriander

¼ tsp ground allspice

¼ tsp chilli powder

Finely grated zest of 1 lime

500g/2½ cups cooked black beans (the equivalent of 2 x 400g tins)

100g/½ cup cooked quinoa (optional)

A small bunch of coriander (cilantro), finely chopped, plus extra to serve

Sea salt and freshly ground black pepper

For the salsa

Finely grated zest of 1 lime and the juice of ½ lime

1 mango or papaya

2 spring onions (scallions), finely chopped

A few sprigs of coriander (cilantro)

For the crema

150ml/10 tbsp soured cream or crème fraîche

Juice of ½ lime

½ tsp smoked chilli powder or paste

I keep these simple by not adding a coating, and by oven-baking them – however, they can be fried if given a dusting of flour, followed by a dip in eggs and a coating of breadcrumbs. I have made the quinoa optional as it isn't essential but it will lighten up the mixture a little.

To make the bean cakes, preheat the oven to 200°C/400°F/Gas mark 6. Heat the oil in a frying pan and sauté the onion and red (bell) pepper until lightly caramelized and softened. Add the garlic and cook for another minute, then stir in the spices and lime zest. Remove from the heat.

Take half the beans and either mash or whiz in a food processor until well broken down, then scrape into a bowl. Very lightly crush the rest of the beans, using a masher, and add these to the other beans along with the contents of the frying pan, the quinoa, if using, and the coriander (cilantro). Season well with salt and pepper, then combine thoroughly. Divide into 12 even-sized patties and arrange on a large baking tray. Brush both sides with olive oil then bake for 12–15 minutes until lightly browned.

While the bean cakes are baking, make the salsa. Put the lime zest and juice into a bowl. Peel the mango or papaya, scraping out the seeds if using papaya, then cut the flesh into dice. Add to the bowl with the spring onions (scallions) and coriander (cilantro), then season well with salt and pepper. Stir together.

Make the crema by stirring together the soured cream or crème fraîche, lime juice and chilli powder along with a generous pinch of salt.

Serve the bean cakes with the salsa and crema and a sprinkling of chopped coriander.

Cured Fish with Lime and Tequila (and Crisp Plantain)

Serves 4

For the cured fish

100g/3 tbsp flaky sea salt

50g/¼ cup soft light brown sugar

½ tsp allspice berries, crushed

½ tsp black peppercorns, crushed

Finely grated zest of 2 limes

50ml/3½ tbsp tequila or rum

1 thick fillet of white fish, around 500–600g/16–18oz

For the salsa

1 mango, finely diced

½ cucumber, peeled and diced

1 red chilli, finely chopped

¼ red onion, finely diced

Finely grated zest and juice of ½ lime

A few mint leaves, finely chopped

1 tsp tequila or rum (optional)

Sea salt and freshly ground black pepper

Curing your own fish gives you a lot of control over how you flavour it. Most of the recipes I have tried use salmon, but I realized that I didn't really want a cold water fish being cured with flavours I associate with the tropics. Instead I use a white fish, which also has the advantage of curing in hours as opposed to days.

Lime is integral to this dish – it's in the cure and the salsa, and stops the plantain (if using) from turning black. If you don't want to make the plantain, serve on tostadas (small rounds of lightly fried tortillas) instead, or simply layer on a plate and pile some of the salsa in the middle.

In a small bowl, mix together the salt, sugar, allspice, peppercorns and lime zest. Sprinkle half of this over the base of a dish large enough to hold the fish. Drizzle the tequila or rum over both sides of the fish, then place on top of the salt and spice mix. Sprinkle over the remaining salt and spice mix. Cover with plastic wrap and leave to cure in the refrigerator for around 6 hours, then rinse thoroughly and pat dry – don't worry, you will not be rinsing off the flavour with the salt; it will have impregnated the flesh. Slice into thin slices at an angle.

For the salsa, mix all the ingredients together in a bowl with a very little salt (the fish will still be quite salty) and some pepper.

To serve, pile the fish onto the plantain (if making, see opposite) or tostadas and top with the salsa.

Juice of 1 lime

2 large, green plantain

Vegetable oil, for deep-frying

For the plantain (optional)

These provide a crisp, nutty base for cured fish and are endlessly versatile – I really like them simply topped with guacamole or some smoked fish. They do not keep well, turning starchy very quickly, so try to eat when still warm.

Put some cold water in a medium bowl and add the lime juice.

Peel (or in practice cut through and break off) the skin from the plantain. Cut into 2cm/¾-in diagonal slices and drop into the water as you go.

Heat enough oil for deep-frying in a large, heavy-based pan or fryer, to about 160°C/320°F. Drain the plantain, then par-fry them in the oil for around 3 minutes, until very lightly coloured and slightly softened.

Remove the plantain to kitchen paper then squash each slice flat under something heavy, such as a heavy-based frying pan; they should be around 0.5cm/¼-in thick with a much larger surface area.

Reheat the oil to around 180°C/350°F. Dip each plantain slice into the limed water, shake off the excess (but don't pat dry; they should be slightly wet) and drop into the hot oil. Fry until they are a rich golden brown, then remove with a slotted spoon and drain on kitchen paper.

Sprouting Broccoli with Blood Orange Hollandaise

Serves 4

50g/⅓ cup hazelnuts

A large bunch of purple sprouting
  broccoli spears, trimmed

A drizzle of olive oil

Sea salt

For the hollandaise

2 egg yolks

Finely grated zest and juice of 1
  blood orange

250g/1 cup plus 2 tbsp clarified
  butter, melted

This hollandaise, also known as *sauce maltaise*, is traditionally paired with asparagus. If you live in the UK and want to eat seasonally, this pairing makes little sense as blood oranges and asparagus aren't available at the same time. Fortunately, I have found that making the dish with sprouting broccoli is even better – in fact, the sauce works well with everything in season in February. Try it also with griddled chicory (endive), leeks, stripped Swiss chard stems – or even calçots.

First make the hollandaise. Fold up a tea towel and place it under a bowl – this will keep the bowl steady when you need to whisk and pour at the same time.

Put the egg yolks in the bowl and add the orange zest with a pinch of salt. Whisk lightly using a balloon whisk. Put most of the orange juice into a small saucepan, reserving a little, and bring to the boil. Remove from the heat, then pour over the egg yolks in a slow, steady stream, whisking as you go. Keep whisking until foamy.

When you have incorporated all the juice, start adding the butter, very gradually and whisking constantly. When the butter has been incorporated you should have a rich, frothy hollandaise. Stir in the reserved orange juice. Keep warm – either by covering the bowl and leaving it over a pan of hot water, or simply transferring to a thermos flask.

Put the hazelnuts in a frying pan and toast over a medium heat, shaking regularly, until aromatic and nutty. Remove from the heat and crush lightly so they break apart.

Blanch the purple sprouting broccoli in boiling water for 2–3 minutes, then drain thoroughly and season with salt.

Meanwhile, heat a griddle pan until very hot. Griddle the sprouting broccoli for a couple of minutes on each side, then pile onto a large platter. Sprinkle with the hazelnuts and either serve with the hollandaise in bowls for dipping, or drizzle it over – how you serve it depends very much on whether or not you want to use your fingers.

Deep-fried Citrus Slices

Serves 4

2–3 citrus fruits (a variety is good)

100ml/7 tbsp buttermilk

75g/generous ½ cup plain (all-purpose) flour

25g/1 tbsp semolina or fine cornmeal

A neutral-tasting oil, such as groundnut or sunflower, for deep-frying

To serve
Pinches of:

Smoked chilli (chipotle) or hot smoked paprika (for lime slices)

Herbes de Provence or za'atar (for orange slices)

Fennel pollen or sumac (for lemon slices)

For the yogurt dip (optional)
250ml/generous 1 cup Greek yogurt

1 tsp fennel seeds, crushed

A pinch of sugar

A squeeze of lemon juice

Sea salt and freshly ground black pepper

The idea for these comes from one of my favourite cookbooks, *The Zuni Café Cookbook* by the late Judy Rodgers. They are so unexpectedly moreish that there is a fine argument for eating them on their own, with just a sprinkle of salt – do try them that way at least once. But there are other things that do enhance the flavour. Lemon is good with a fine sprinkling of sumac or fennel pollen, lime loves a dash of smoked chilli or cayenne, whilst orange I like with herbes de Provence or za'atar.

I don't always bother with an accompaniment for these, but when I do, I make this yogurt dip. You can replace the fennel with any of the flavour suggestions mentioned above, or indeed anything else you fancy.

If serving with the dip, make this first – simply mix everything together and season with salt and pepper.

Top and tail the citrus fruit to the point where you get a good showing of flesh as opposed to pith and skin. Slice the fruit as finely as possible while keeping each slice intact, removing any pips.

Put the buttermilk in a bowl. Put the flour and semolina onto a plate and season with salt and pepper, then whisk briefly to combine and get rid of any lumps.

Dip the citrus slices in the buttermilk and shake or lightly scrape them to get rid of any excess. Drop the slices onto the flour mixture and give the plate a little shake. Flip over and repeat. Dust off any excess – you don't want a thick coating as you want to see the detail from the citrus through the batter.

Heat enough oil for deep-frying in a heavy-based saucepan or fryer to about 180°C/350°F. Fry the slices a few at a time – when they start to go golden brown remove with a slotted spoon to a plate lined with kitchen paper. The slices will continue to brown once they are removed and will be nicely caramelized in patches.

Sprinkle with salt, then the corresponding spices and/or herbs for each fruit and serve with yogurt dip, if you like.

Sea Bass Ceviche

Serves 4

2 small, sweet oranges

1 small red onion, thinly sliced

600g/1lb 5oz extremely fresh sea bass, placed in the freezer for 30 minutes

100g/3½oz small tomatoes, preferably yellow/orange, cut into quarters

A few small coriander (cilantro) leaves

A few small basil leaves

For the tiger's milk

2.5cm/1-in piece of fresh root ginger, sliced

1 fat garlic clove, squashed

A few coriander (cilantro) stems, bruised

100ml/7 tbsp lime juice (or sour orange juice)

½ Scotch bonnet chilli, finely chopped, plus extra to serve

A few thyme sprigs, bruised

Sea salt

Note on fish

I prefer clean-tasting sea bass or bream for ceviche, but use whatever is freshest on the day. Just don't use anything that is liable to flake, and bear in mind that any firmer fish will need to marinate for a little longer.

One period of my working life was spent researching Peruvian food, and out of this came a mild obsession with what is known as "tigre de leche", or tiger's milk. This is a purée of citrus and chilli that is used to "cook" the fish to its ceviched state – the remains are often drunk in shot glasses or used in cocktails. Lime is the usual citrus in ceviche, but you can also use sour orange juice.

This recipe has a Caribbean flavour, as I love the taste and aroma of Scotch bonnet chillies.

Segment the oranges (see page 15), working over a bowl to catch any juice, cut each segment in half and set aside. Squeeze out the peel and membranes into the juice.

Next make the tiger's milk. Put the ginger and garlic in a small bowl with the coriander (cilantro) stems, lime juice, chilli and thyme. Add the reserved juice and leave for 5 minutes to infuse. Strain, then add a generous pinch of salt.

Put some iced water in a small bowl with a teaspoon of salt added. Add the red onion and leave to soak for 5 minutes. Drain and dry.

To prepare the sea bass, place it skin side down, then cut thin slices diagonally across the grain so you end up with fairly flat, skinless slices, similar to the way you would cut smoked salmon. Cut these in half. Alternatively, you can simply cut into thick strips, but I think the slices look prettier on the plate. Put in a bowl, sprinkle with a generous pinch of salt, and mix. After 2 minutes, add the tiger's milk and leave for a further 2 minutes only (it will carry on "cooking" after being removed).

Remove the sea bass from its marinade and arrange flat on a plate. Add the red onion slices, orange segments and tomatoes, then sprinkle with the cilantro (cilantro) and basil. Serve immediately, with shots of the leftover marinade on the side if you like.

Salmon Tiradito with Yuzu

Serves 4

4 spring onions (scallions), green
  part only

400g/14oz best-quality salmon fillet,
  skinned and well chilled

50g/1¾oz cucumber, deseeded and
  finely diced

A few sprigs of cress

A few sprigs of dill

A few black sesame seeds

For the dressing

2 tbsp yuzu juice

½ tsp powdered yuzu zest (optional)

Finely grated zest and juice of 1 lime

50g/1¾oz cucumber, peeled and
  deseeded

1 garlic clove, peeled and squashed

1cm/½-in piece of fresh root
  ginger, peeled

2 tbsp mirin

½ tbsp dark soy sauce

1 tsp sugar

1 green chilli, such as jalapeño,
  roughly chopped

A tiradito is a hybrid dish, as it is a cross between Japanese sashimi and Peruvian ceviche. The dressing is like a hot yet cooling ponzu, thanks to the addition of cucumber, and can be used to dress anything. Don't limit it to oily fish – try over grilled meat or vegetables too.

First make the dressing. Put all the ingredients into a small food processor and blitz until fairly smooth. It is up to you whether you strain it or not – I quite like it green-flecked. Taste and adjust the salt, sugar and citrus juice if you feel the balance is not quite right – some limes are sweeter/less acidic than others.

Cut the spring onion (scallion) greens into 6cm/2½-in lengths. Cut down one side to open up, then shred lengthways. Put into a bowl of iced water until they curl up – it will take at least 30 minutes. Drain thoroughly.

Cut the salmon into slices similar to the cut of smoked salmon – so as finely as you can across the grain into thin slices that span the width of the fish. Arrange over 4 serving plates and sprinkle over the cucumber, cress, dill and spring onion curls. Drizzle over the dressing and sprinkle with the sesame seeds.

Bruschetta with Citrus Labneh, Broad Beans and Za'atar

Serves 4

4 slices of sourdough bread

Olive oil, to drizzle

4 tbsp broad beans (fava beans), blanched and skinned

A sprinkling each of za'atar and sumac

A drizzle of liquid from quick cheat's lemons (optional, see page 22)

For the labneh

500ml/2 cups full fat Greek yogurt

½ tsp salt

Finely grated zest of 1 lemon

Finely grated zest of 1 mandarin or lime

½ tsp finely chopped rosemary

At a pinch, you could use a good curd cheese for this instead of making labneh, if you are in a hurry. But making your own does give beautifully creamy results.

To make the labneh, mix the yogurt with the salt in a bowl. Line a sieve or colander with a double layer of muslin or cheesecloth. Place the yoghurt in the muslin, bring up the sides of the cloth and tie them together. Either suspend the cloth from a wooden spoon or leave in a large colander, both placed over a bowl to catch any liquid. Leave in the refrigerator overnight, then transfer the labneh to a bowl and stir in the zests and herbs.

To assemble, toast the bread and drizzle with olive oil. Slather some of the labneh quite thickly onto the bread. Sprinkle with the broad (fava) beans, za'atar and sumac, then drizzle over the preserved lemon liquid, if using, and more olive oil.

Grilled Prawns with Curried Lime and Garlic Butter

Serves 4

100g/scant ½ cup butter

Finely grated zest of 2 limes

3 garlic cloves, crushed

½ Scotch bonnet chilli, very finely chopped

½ tsp Caribbean curry powder

1 tsp fresh thyme leaves, finely chopped

1kg/2lb 3oz shell-on prawns (shrimp), split down the middle but with heads still attached

2 limes, cut into quarters

Sea salt and freshly ground black pepper

I do this the Caribbean way and add a pinch of curry powder to the butter, but don't feel bound by this – you can make a more versatile butter without. This is also good made with split lobster tails or langoustine.

Heat a large griddle pan or barbecue. Melt the butter with the lime zest, garlic, chilli, curry powder and thyme, then season with plenty of salt and pepper. Flatten out the prawns (shrimp) and brush with a little of the flavoured butter, then grill cut side down for a couple of minutes. Turn over and brush with more of the butter mixture and grill for a further 2 minutes.

Remove to a plate and add the limes to the griddle or barbecue. Cook for around 30 seconds on each cut side to caramelize and char slightly.

Serve with the rest of the flavoured butter for dipping, and the lime wedges for squeezing.

Lemon Pizzette

Makes 12 small or 8 large

For the dough
500g/3½–3⅔ cups strong white flour,
   plus extra for dusting
7g/¼oz instant dried yeast
10g/2 tsp salt
300ml/1¼ cups warm water
2 tbsp olive oil

For the meat topping
Fresh mozzarella, shredded
Very thinly sliced lemon
Italian fennel sausages, skinned
Dried chilli flakes (red pepper flakes)
Fresh basil leaves
Olive oil

Vegetarian variation
**Substitute the fennel
sausages for thinly sliced
artichoke hearts.**

The lemon and fennel combination here is one that
appears frequently throughout this book, in both
savoury and sweet dishes – they work so well together.
Fennel is also wonderful with orange, so you can
substitute if you like.

It doesn't make sense to make a smaller amount of
dough, but you can freeze any you don't use – just wrap
it into individual portions after it has risen and place in
the freezer. Transfer to the refrigerator the night before
you want to use it (or in the morning, for evening use)
so it can defrost slowly, then proceed as normal.

To make the dough, mix the flour and yeast together in
a large bowl, then add the salt. Gradually add the water
and olive oil until you have a dough, then turn out onto a
floured surface and knead until the dough is soft, smooth
and elastic. (Alternatively, put the whole lot in a stand
mixer and mix and knead with the dough hook.) Return to
the bowl, cover with a damp tea towel or plastic wrap and
leave until it has doubled in size.

For small pizzette (around 20cm/8-in diameter) divide the
dough into 12 balls. For larger, 30cm/12-in pizzette, divide
into 8. (Freeze any dough you are not using at this stage.)

Preheat your oven to its highest temperature. Preheat a
pizza stone or baking tray/s.

Roll out each piece of dough to the desired size, pulling
it out until it stops springing back. Add some shredded
mozzarella. Blanch the lemon slices (allowing for a couple
per pizzetta) in boiling water for 1 minute, then drain
and cut into quarters. Arrange over the mozzarella, then
crumble over the fennel sausages. Sprinkle over a few chilli
flakes (red pepper flakes) and basil leaves, then drizzle
with olive oil.

Transfer the pizzette to the preheated stone or baking
trays, working in batches if necessary, and bake for
6–8 minutes. Serve immediately, sprinkled with extra
basil leaves.

Lemon- and Salt-Cooked Potatoes with Saffron Aioli

Serves 4

1kg/2lb 3oz new, salad or waxy potatoes, preferably quite small, scrubbed but unpeeled

30g/1 tbsp flaky sea salt (Maldon is good, as is the smoked version for a slightly different flavour)

Finely grated zest of 2 lemons

1 tsp herbes de Provence

½ tsp black peppercorns, freshly ground or crushed

1 litre/generous 4 cups water

For the aioli

A large pinch of saffron strands

1 tbsp warm water

3 garlic cloves, crushed

2 egg yolks

½ tsp Dijon mustard

A pinch of salt

300ml/1¼ cups sunflower oil

Juice of ½ lemon

The idea for this came out of a love of salt-crusted potatoes which I thought could benefit from a bit of extra flavour. The zest and saffron will cling to the salt and therefore also the outside of the potatoes – a good contrast to the creamy aioli.

Put the potatoes in a large, heavy-based frying pan (I use one with straight, fairly deep sides), making sure they fit in a single layer. Mix the salt with the zest, herbes de Provence and pepper. Add to the potatoes with the water.

Bring the water to the boil and, rather than turn down to simmer, keep boiling until the liquid has evaporated. When all the water has disappeared, turn the heat down low and cook for a few minutes, giving the pan a shake every so often to roll the potatoes over, until they are completely dry and wrinkly with a light coating of flavoured salt.

While they are cooking, make the aioli. Using a pestle and mortar, grind the saffron strands to a powder, spoon the warm water over and set aside to soak. Fold up a tea towel and place it under a bowl – this will keep the bowl steady when you need to whisk and pour at the same time.

Put the crushed garlic in the bowl with the egg yolks, mustard and saffron-infused water. Add the salt, then whisk, using a balloon whisk, until completely combined. Start drizzling in the oil, a drop at a time and whisking all the time until you are confident the mixture has emulsified, then you can add it at a slightly faster rate. Continue until all the oil has been incorporated, then add the lemon juice. Give a final whisk – it will look liquid for a minute but will soon settle back into a thick, creamy mayonnaise.

Serve the potatoes hot from the pan. They should be the perfect combination of zesty, salty crust and sweet flesh; perfect with the aioli.

Yuzu Prawn Cocktail

Serves 4

250g/9oz large, cooked, peeled
  prawns (shrimp)

½ tsp sea salt

A pinch of ground white pepper

½ tsp powdered yuzu zest, plus a little
  extra to serve (optional)

1 heart of Romaine lettuce, shredded,
  or other salad greens

For the dressing

50g/scant ¼ cup Greek yogurt

50g/scant ¼ cup mayonnaise

2 tbsp yuzu juice

1 tsp powdered yuzu zest (optional)

¼ tsp runny honey

¼ tsp wasabi

¼ tsp chilli sauce (preferably a
  green one)

A few snips of dill, plus extra to serve
  (optional)

Sea salt and freshly ground black
  pepper

As much as I love a classic, British prawn cocktail, there is something to be said for lightening it up. The flavours here nod towards the spicier, American version, but the recipe uses yuzu and a hint of wasabi instead of lemon and horseradish. Coating the prawns (shrimp) in yuzu flavoured salt is not essential, but adds an extra tang and offsets their sweetness nicely.

You can use any lettuce leaves here – I really like the crunch of a Romaine or Cos, but will usually supplement it with a bitter note from a curly radicchio or similar.

Put the prawns (shrimp) in a bowl. Using a pestle and mortar, grind together the salt, white pepper and yuzu zest, if using, and sprinkle the mixture over the prawns. Divide the lettuce between 4 serving bowls or glasses.

Whisk all the dressing ingredients together, with some salt and pepper. Taste and adjust the flavours accordingly. Add the prawns to the lettuce leaves and top with some of the dressing. Garnish with a little more yuzu powder and a few snips of dill, if you like.

Tuna, Orange and Beetroot Poke

Serves 4

2 oranges or 4 mandarins

400g/14oz extremely fresh well-chilled tuna, or other oily fish

2 medium-sized cooked beetroot (beets), peeled and diced

1 avocado, diced

2 spring onions (scallions), finely chopped

Sea salt

For the dressing

1 garlic clove, finely chopped

2 tbsp finely chopped coriander (cilantro) stems (save the leaves for serving)

Finely grated zest of 1 lime

Finely grated zest of 1 mandarin (optional – only if the proper ones are in season)

2cm/¾-in piece of fresh root ginger, peeled and grated

1 red chilli, finely chopped

2 tbsp light soy sauce

A dash of brown rice vinegar

A few drops of sesame oil

To serve

Juice of 1 lime

Cooked sushi rice or quinoa, or a few lettuce leaves

Sesame seeds

A handful of coriander (cilantro) leaves

In a classic poke (pronounced po-kay), any very acidic citrus is almost incidental and added at the last minute as the fish should be raw, not "cooked". I have taken some of the classic elements and added beetroot (beet), as I like its sweet, earthy flavours here. You don't have to use tuna – any oily fish would work, including mackerel.

Segment the oranges or mandarins (see page 15) over a bowl to catch any juice, and set the segments aside. Squeeze out the peel and membranes into the juice.

Make sure the tuna is extremely well chilled – in fact, it does no harm to freeze it for an hour before you want to use it, and makes it easier to cut. Cut into an even dice, around 1.5–2cm/½–¾-in, place in a dish and sprinkle with salt. Whisk together all the dressing ingredients and pour over the tuna. Leave to marinate in the refrigerator for 30–60 minutes, no longer.

When you are ready to serve, put the tuna and its dressing in a serving bowl with the orange or mandarin segments, beetroot (beet), avocado and spring onions (scallions). Mix the reserved juice with the lime juice and pour over the contents of the bowl. Fold very gently – you don't want the beetroot to bleed too much or for the avocado to turn to mush.

Serve with rice (traditional) or quinoa, or simply pile into lettuce leaves, sprinkled with sesame seeds and coriander (cilantro) leaves.

Grilled Chard Stems with Lemon and Anchovy Sauce

Serves 4

Juice of ½ lemon

A large bunch of fairly mature Swiss chard, stripped of leaves and stems cut into 10cm/4-in lengths

1 tbsp olive oil

Sea salt and freshly ground black pepper

For the sauce

100g/7 tbsp butter

1 x 50g/2oz tin of anchovies in olive oil

Finely grated zest and juice of 1 lemon

2 garlic cloves, crushed

½ tsp dried chilli flakes (red pepper flakes), optional

Another highly calorific sauce here to make eating a pile of vegetables much less worthy. I could quite happily live on this kind of dish – throw in some bread for mopping at the end and you've just about covered all food groups. Add a few capers as well if you like.

Add the lemon juice to a bowl of water. Drop the chard stems into the acidulated water to stop them from going brown.

Heat a griddle pan to a medium heat – you don't want it as hot as you would for meat. Drain the chard stems, shake off any excess water and rub with the oil. Sprinkle with salt and pepper and place on the griddle. Grill on both sides until softened, with distinctive char lines.

Meanwhile, make the sauce. Put the butter and anchovies, including their oil, in a small saucepan. Set over a low heat and when the butter has melted set to work on the anchovies, mashing them into the butter and oil. Add the lemon zest and juice, garlic and chilli (red pepper) flakes, if using. Taste (as the anchovies are salty) and add seasoning if you think it needs it. Give it a good whisk just to stop any separation in its tracks. Serve the chard with the sauce in a bowl on the side. Use your fingers and dip the chard, or be more decorous and pour the sauce over, to be eaten with a knife and fork.

Citrus-Glazed Chicken Wings

Serves 4

1kg/2lb 3oz chicken wings, tips cut off

A few spring onions (scallions), green
parts only

A few sesame seeds, to sprinkle
(optional)

Sea salt and freshly ground black
pepper

For the marinade

50ml/3½ tbsp light soy sauce

50ml/3½ tbsp rum

½ onion, roughly chopped

Finely grated zest and juice of 1 lime

Juice of 1 orange

2 garlic cloves, roughly chopped

5cm/2-in piece of fresh root ginger,
peeled and roughly chopped

1 red chilli, roughly chopped

For the glaze

½ tsp finely chopped grapefruit zest
and juice of 1 grapefruit

50g/3½ tbsp butter

2 tsp runny honey

½ tsp chilli powder

1 tbsp light soy sauce

1 tsp rum

I have been making these wings for so long and so
frequently that it sometimes feels like the ingredients
just walk themselves into my marinating bowl –
I don't have to think about it. You can of course alter
the flavours as you see fit – not everyone will want
grapefruit zest in the glaze, so you can use sour orange
or lime in its place.

If you want to split the wings into flats and drummettes,
you can do so, otherwise leave them in their natural heart
shape. Put into a bowl and season with salt and pepper.
Put all the marinade ingredients into a food processor and
blend together until smooth. Pour over the chicken wings
and stir to combine – give a massage with your hands if
you can bear to; it will make a difference. Leave for at least
an hour, but up to overnight (refrigerated) if possible.

When you are ready to cook, either prepare a barbecue or
preheat the oven to 200°C/400°F/Gas mark 6.

For the glaze, put the grapefruit juice into a small
saucepan over a high heat and reduce by half. Add the
butter and honey. When melted, whisk in the zest, chilli
powder, soy sauce and rum. Drain the chicken wings and
pat dry. Either grill over indirect heat, turning regularly
and basting with the glaze, or spread them out on baking
tray, brush with the glaze and bake in the oven for around
45–50 minutes, turning and basting with the glaze
regularly, until a rich dark brown with crisp, slightly
sticky skin.

Meanwhile, cut the spring onion (scallion) greens into
lengths and cut down one side to open up, then shred
lengthways. Put into a bowl of iced water until they
curl up pleasingly – it will take at least half an hour.
Drain thoroughly.

To serve, sprinkle the spring onion greens over the wings
with some sesame seeds, if you like.

Salads

There are very few days in our house that don't have meals involving some kind of salad, and most of these will include citrus in one form or another, even if it is just by way of a quick whisk of olive oil and lemon juice. Citrus take us through the seasons – limes pretty much all year round, lemons from spring through to autumn, and all types of oranges and mandarins throughout the winter months. At one point I used to consider citrus in winter as a replacement for tomatoes, and it is true that oranges feature more heavily in my salads when good tomatoes are scarce. But I was excited to discover how wonderful lemons and tomatoes can be together – each brings out the sweetness in the other as well as providing some acidic balance.

The recipes in this chapter more than in any of the others are real snapshots for me – salad at home is never the same twice. It is usually a case of opening the refrigerator – or in summer, if I've been organized, strolling down to the bottom of the garden to the raised beds – to see what needs using up and what might work well together. It also means that the recipes can be quite elusive and hard to pin down when it comes to writing them up, which is why recently I could be found on the telephone pleading with a friend to recall exactly what it was I had put in the lobster salad. So in this chapter above all others I cannot be prescriptive. Please use the recipes to inspire: do not feel you must follow each one to the letter.

Lobster Salad with Quinoa, Avocado, Mango and Citrus Dressing

Serves 4

15g/1 tbsp butter or olive oil

1 garlic clove, crushed

½ tsp smoked chilli powder

Finely grated zest and juice of ½ lime

2 cooked lobsters or 4 lobster tails,
  meat roughly chopped

2 oranges

1 large Cos or Romaine heart, shredded

100g/½ cup cooked quinoa (about
  30g/⅕ cup raw)

2 avocados, diced

4 spring onions (scallions), shredded

A small bunch of coriander (cilantro)

A small bunch of basil

Sea salt

For the dressing

½ very ripe mango, peeled and diced

Finely grated zest and juice of ½ lime

1cm/½-in piece of fresh root ginger,
  peeled and grated

The lobster isn't mandatory here – you could use any kind of shellfish – but do make sure you get something plump, sweet and buttery rather than mushy and waterlogged.

Melt the butter or heat the oil in a frying pan. Add the garlic and sauté for 2–3 minutes, just to soften and take the edge off its astringency. Add the chilli powder along with the lime zest and juice. Season with plenty of salt, then whisk together. Remove from the heat and add the lobster meat. Turn over lightly so the lobster is well coated in the flavoured butter.

Segment the oranges (see page 15) over a bowl to catch any juices, then squeeze the membranes and peel over the bowl to extract more juice. Arrange the segments with all the other salad ingredients, including the lobster, over a large platter, drizzling over the buttery juices as well. Whisk together the dressing ingredients with some salt, then drop spoonfuls of this over the lobster. Serve immediately.

Blood Orange, Burrata
and Freekeh Salad

Serves 4

100g/⅔ cup freekeh

600ml/2½ cups chicken or
  vegetable stock

2 garlic cloves, finely chopped

1 tsp finely grated bergamot zest
  (or lemon zest)

Juice of ½ bergamot (or lemon)

1 tbsp olive oil, plus extra for drizzling

2 small red onions, sliced vertically
  into thin wedges

A large bunch of chard, shredded

50ml/3½ tbsp water

2 large blood or blush oranges, peeled
  and sliced, any juice squeezed from
  the peel reserved

1 large or 2 small burrata

A handful of mint leaves

Sea salt and freshly ground black
  pepper

**This is a very happy confluence of ingredients; smoky
nuttiness from the freekeh, earthiness from the chard,
a creamy sweetness from the burrata, all pulled together
by the fragrant, sweet-sour citrus. The bergamot is
purely optional as its flavour is subtle here, but if you
can, please do: bergamots are still in season (just) when
blood oranges come in, so it should be possible to find
them. Use lemon zest instead if not.**

First cook the freekeh. Soak it in plenty of cold water
for 5 minutes, then drain and rinse thoroughly. Put in a
medium saucepan with the stock, garlic and zest. Season
with salt, then bring to the boil and leave to simmer for
15–20 minutes until cooked – it should be plumped up
but still with some bite. Add the bergamot juice and leave
to stand for a few minutes before straining.

Heat the olive oil in a large frying pan. Add the onion
wedges and sauté over a medium heat until starting
to turn translucent – you want them softened but not
completely collapsed. Add the chard, along with the water,
and cook over a gentle heat until the chard has wilted
down and the stems are still al dente. Season with salt
and pepper.

Arrange the freekeh over a large platter and top with the
onions and chard. Pour over any reserved juice from the
blood oranges – there should be a fair bit. Break up the
burrata over the salad, then top with the orange slices and
mint leaves. Drizzle over a little olive oil.

Marinated Squid, Smoked Chilli, Fennel and Lemon Salad

Serves 4

60ml/¼ cup olive oil

Finely grated zest and juice of 1 lemon

1 tsp ouzo (optional)

Pinch of caster (superfine) sugar

½–1 tsp smoked chilli powder or paste (such as chipotle)

400g/14oz squid, cleaned and cut into rings, tentacles included

2 garlic cloves, finely chopped

200g/7oz new potatoes, boiled in their skins, kept warm then sliced (optional)

1 fennel bulb, finely sliced

1 lemon, segmented (see page 15), or use orange if you prefer

2 red chillies, finely sliced (deseeded for less heat if you like)

Leaves from small bunches of parsley, Greek basil (the small-leaved stuff if you can get it, otherwise regular basil) and oregano

Sea salt and freshly ground black pepper

There are two ways to cook squid quickly. The methods with which most people are familiar involve grilling and frying, which have to be done last minute. The advantage of the method in this recipe is all in the timing – you can blanch the squid, then leave it in its marinade until you need to serve it. This makes it the perfect, prepare-ahead salad. Just make sure that if you leave it to marinate in the refrigerator, you give it enough time to return to room temperature before you serve it.

In a large bowl, whisk together the olive oil, lemon zest and juice, ouzo, if using, sugar and chilli powder or paste. Add salt and pepper to taste.

Bring a large saucepan of salted water to the boil. When it is nicely rolling, add all the squid and garlic and boil for precisely 40 seconds. Drain and immediately add to the prepared marinade.

Leave the squid to marinate for at least an hour, then mix with the new potatoes, if using, fennel and lemon. Add the chillies, parsley, basil and oregano and toss everything gently together. Serve at room temperature.

Pomelo and Crab Salad with Candied Cashew Nuts

Serves 4

1 pomelo or 2 grapefruit

½ Chinese cabbage, shredded

½ green papaya, grated

1 carrot, julienned

½ jicama (Mexican yam) or 1
  Jerusalem artichoke, or 1 green apple,
  peeled and julienned

200g/7oz white crab meat

A few sprigs of coriander (cilantro)

For the candied cashew nuts

2 tbsp maple syrup

100g/generous ¾ cup cashew nuts

Pinch of smoked paprika

Pinch of smoked salt

For the dressing

1 shallot, finely sliced

1 tbsp neutral tasting oil, such
  as sunflower or groundnut

Juice of 1 lime

1 tbsp light soy sauce

½ tsp runny honey

Sea salt (optional)

You can use grapefruit in this salad instead of pomelo if you prefer – I use them interchangeably. The grapefruit, even the pink or ruby ones, will have bitter notes not found in the pomelo. Jicamas are still relatively scarce in the UK, but can be found in any oriental supermarket, for a price. They are a type of yam, with a crisp, Granny Smith taste and texture, but with savoury notes.

For the candied cashew nuts, put the maple syrup in a frying pan, add the cashew nuts and cook over a medium heat, stirring constantly, until the maple syrup first turns sticky, then powdery. Remove from the heat and add the paprika and smoked salt. Toss to combine and turn out onto a plate or board to cool. Set aside.

Segment the pomelo or grapefruit (see page 15) over a bowl to catch any juice, and set aside. Squeeze out the peel and membranes into the juice and reserve.

Assemble the salad by gently mixing the pomelo or grapefruit segments with the cabbage, papaya, carrot and jicama (or artichoke or apple).

Whisk the dressing ingredients together and taste, adding a little salt if necessary. Add the reserved juice, then use to dress the salad. Top with the crab, coriander (cilantro) and candied cashew nuts.

Feta, Cantaloupe and Lime Salad

Serves 4

1 medium-sized ripe cantaloupe melon

1 cucumber

1 lime

250g/9oz feta, cut into chunks

A handful of mint leaves

For the dressing

1 tbsp olive oil

1 tsp white wine vinegar

Finely grated zest and juice of 1 lime

1 tsp runny honey

½ tsp ground cardamom

5g/⅙oz fresh root ginger, peeled and grated

Sea salt and freshly ground black pepper

The success of this salad is very dependent on the quality of the melon – you will need a sweet, fragrant one to give contrast to the sharpness of the lime. If you can't get a ripe one, use watermelon, which is usually more reliably sweet. Whilst I will eat this on its own, it is also a good foil for anything spicy or particularly rich. You can also bake the feta if you like, to give a creamier flavour. Just cut it into squares and bake at 200°C/400°F/Gas mark 6 for around 10 minutes.

Quarter the melon, peel and deseed, then cut into chunks and put into a bowl. Peel the cucumber, cut in half lengthways and scrape out the seeds with a teaspoon. Slice each half into chunky crescents, about 0.5cm/¼-in thick, and add to the melon. Cut the skin away from the lime (see page 15) and slice into thin rounds, then add to the bowl.

Make the dressing by whisking all the ingredients together and seasoning with salt and pepper. Drizzle most of the dressing over the melon, cucumber and lime salad, and toss well.

Arrange the salad over 4 serving plates and add the feta. Sprinkle over some mint leaves and top with more dressing.

Coconut, Lime and Lemongrass Chicken Salad

Serves 4

For the chicken

1 tbsp coconut oil

6 boneless chicken thighs or 4 breasts, skin on

4 garlic cloves, finely sliced

2 thin slices of fresh root ginger, peeled and chopped

3 lemongrass stalks, outer leaves discarded, finely chopped

1 x 400ml tin/1¾ cups coconut milk

Finely grated zest and juice of 2 limes

2 kaffir lime leaves, shredded (optional)

1 tbsp fish sauce

Sea salt and crushed white peppercorns

Handfuls of mint, coriander (cilantro) and basil, to serve

For the salad

2 tbsp vegetable oil

2 shallots, finely sliced

1 large carrot, peeled and julienned

1 large courgette (zucchini), julienned

100g/1⅓ cups cauliflower florets, finely sliced

A small bunch of radishes, finely sliced

A bunch of spring onions (scallions), finely sliced on the diagonal

For the dressing

A small piece of fresh root ginger, peeled and grated

1 red chilli, finely chopped

Finely grated zest and juice of 1 lime

1 tbsp fish sauce

In keeping with many Thai dishes, the citrus notes in this salad are sweet and fragrant, with most of the bite coming from the ginger and chilli.

First prepare the chicken. Heat the coconut oil in a large, shallow pan and add the chicken, skin side down. Fry on a medium to high heat until the skin is crisp and brown, then turn over. Add the garlic, ginger and lemongrass, then pour the coconut milk around the chicken. Add the lime zest and juice, the lime leaves, if using, and the peppercorns, and season with the fish sauce and some salt. Reduce the heat and leave to simmer, uncovered so the sauce reduces, until the chicken is cooked through, around 15 minutes. Remove the chicken. Strain the sauce and reserve.

To assemble the salad, heat the vegetable oil in a small pan and fry the shallots quite briskly until they are translucent and well browned. Remove to drain on some kitchen paper and set aside. Arrange the raw vegetables over a large plate or platter. Slice or shred the chicken, skin included, and add to the vegetables.

Whisk all the dressing ingredients together with 4 tablespoons of the reserved cooking sauce, and pour over the salad. Sprinkle with the herbs and the fried shallots.

Beef Carpaccio Salad with Lemon-Mandarin-kosho dressing

Serves 4

500g/1lb 2oz piece of beef fillet

A handful of shiso leaves (optional)

A handful of lamb's lettuce leaves

A handful of watercress or landcress leaves

A few radishes, finely chopped

A few black sesame seeds

1 orange, segmented (see page 15) and diced

For the carpaccio dressing

2 egg yolks

1–2 tsp lemon-mandarin-kosho (see page 24), to taste

2 tbsp mandarin or orange juice

1 tbsp lemon juice

A pinch of sugar

75–100ml/5–7 tbsp olive oil

Sea salt and freshly ground black pepper

For the salad dressing

½ tsp sesame oil

1 red chilli, finely chopped

1 tbsp mandarin or orange juice

1 tsp white wine vinegar

½ tsp runny honey

A beef carpaccio will usually have a dressing similar to a thin mayonnaise. This follows that tradition, but adds the kosho, which really helps to ramp up the savoury qualities of the dish. If you don't have any kosho made up, you can add some very finely chopped preserved citrus and fresh chilli to the dressing instead.

First prepare the beef for slicing. Wrap it tightly in plastic wrap and put in the freezer for at least 30 minutes, preferably a little longer (up to an hour), to firm it up.

Meanwhile, make the dressings. For the carpaccio dressing, put the egg yolks, kosho and juices in a bowl and whisk together with the sugar. Gradually drizzle in the oil, initially a few drops at a time, until you have a fairly thin emulsion. You may not need to use all the oil. Taste for seasoning and add salt, pepper or more sugar if you think it needs it. Set aside.

Whisk together the salad dressing ingredients and season with salt and pepper. Set to one side.

Prepare the beef. Remove the plastic wrap, then using your sharpest knife, slice as thinly as you can. Arrange over 4 serving plates and drizzle with the carpaccio dressing, making sure you reserve some of it.

Put all the salad leaves in a bowl and drizzle over the salad dressing. Mix then put a small pile of leaves on top of the carpaccio, then add the radish and orange. Sprinkle with sesame seeds.

Lamb Salad with Artichokes, Preserved Lemons, Dates and Saffron

Serves 2

1 tbsp olive oil

200g/7oz roast lamb, torn into strips

A jar of roast artichokes, rinsed
and sliced

2 small preserved lemons, quartered,
peel finely diced, or 2 tbsp quick
preserved lemon zest (see page 22)

A medium bag of lamb's lettuce

3–4 fat, squishy dates, finely chopped

A handful of mint leaves

For the dressing

A large pinch of saffron strands

1 tbsp hot water from the kettle

1 tsp runny honey

100ml/7 tbsp Greek yogurt

1 garlic clove, crushed

Juice of 1 lemon

2 tbsp olive oil

Sea salt

This is a very good way to use up some roast lamb. If you don't have any, you can grill and thinly slice a couple of lamb steaks – just make sure you let them rest for 10 minutes once you have cooked them. To make this salad more substantial, you could add cooked chickpeas (garbanzo beans) or giant couscous. I love how the sweet lamb and dates contrast with the preserved lemon and saffron, but I have also made this with pomegranates instead of dates to accentuate the sour notes. Very different, but just as good.

Heat the olive oil in a frying pan and add the lamb with a splash of water, just to warm it through and to melt any fat that might be clinging to it. Drain on some kitchen paper.

In a bowl, toss the artichokes with the preserved lemon. Arrange the lamb's lettuce over a platter and top with the lamb and artichokes. Sprinkle over the chopped dates.

Using a pestle and mortar, finely grind the saffron strands with a pinch of salt, then dissolve in the hot water and honey. Whisk into the yogurt with the garlic, lemon juice and olive oil. Taste for seasoning and add more salt if necessary.

Drizzle the bright yellow dressing over the salad, then top with the mint leaves.

Short Salads

Orange and Beetroot Salad with a Ginger Dressing

I would normally put mustard in a dressing for beetroot (beet), but using ginger works very well with the orange and the peppery watercress.

Trim 4 medium-sized cooked beetroots (beets) and cut into wedges. Cut the peel and membranes away from 2 oranges (see page 15) and slice into rounds. Whisk together 1 tbsp oil, 1 tsp brown rice vinegar, juice of ½ lime, 1 tsp dark soy sauce, 1 tsp runny honey, 5g/⅙oz grated root ginger and a few drops of sesame oil. Season with salt and pepper. Arrange the beetroot and orange over a generous pile of watercress and drizzle over the dressing.

Puntarelle and Orange Salad

This is my favourite salad to eat over Christmas. I prefer using bright, sweet navel oranges, but it is also good with blood oranges later in the season. You could get away with a few pomegranate seeds with this or, to make it more substantial, serve it with some slices of smoked meat – duck is particularly good. And if you can't find puntarelle, any type of chicory (endive) or radicchio will work well – it is the bitter notes and the crisp texture you are after. You can also use finely sliced fennel to change the emphasis from bitter to sweet.

Trim off the spears from 1 large head of puntarelle, working towards the middle. You want mainly white stems and fronds here, so discard those that are dark green. Cut into thin slices on the diagonal and put into a large bowl of cold water. Leave to soak for a couple of hours. Cut the peel and membranes from 2 large oranges (see page 15) and cut into slices, flicking out the pips as you go. Juice another orange and mix with 2 tbsp hazelnut or walnut oil, 1 tsp mustard and 1 tbsp lemon juice. Whisk together and season with salt and pepper. Drain the puntarelle and arrange on a serving plate (it will have curled up attractively) with the orange slices, and drizzle over the dressing.

Avocado Vinaigrette

This is a modern version of the classic Italian trattoria dish, in which an avocado "boat" is drenched in vinaigrette. Here the dressing is very hot/salty/sour which I think is perfect with buttery avocado. If you don't have any lime-kosho made up, substitute with the finely grated zest of 1 lime and 1 finely chopped chilli.

Gently heat 2 tbsp olive oil. Add 2 tsp lime-Scotch-bonnet-kosho (see page 26) along with 1 garlic clove and 1 small piece of fresh root ginger, both finely chopped, and 1 tbsp finely chopped coriander (cilantro) stems. Remove from the heat, add the juice of ½ a lime and season with salt and pepper. Cut an avocado in half, remove the stone and peel. Slice each half into lengths and fan over a plate. Segment 1 orange (see page 15) and dice the flesh. Sprinkle this over the avocado. Top with 2 finely chopped spring onion (scallions), then cover with the dressing.

Tomato, Lemon and Caper Salad

Surprising flavours here – the lemon sweetens as it cooks, and it caramelizes, ending up with a piquant sweet/sour flavour that is a surprising match for sweet, ripe tomatoes. For the full impact of this, try without the capers the first time you make it.

Take a large punnet of sweet cherry tomatoes and cut each in half. Arrange over a plate and season with salt. Heat 1 tbsp olive oil in a frying pan. Segment 1 large lemon (see page 15), dice and strain, reserving the juice for something else. Add the lemon to the hot oil, along with 1 tbsp capers. It should spit and sizzle. Toss a couple of times, then pour the lot over the tomatoes. Sprinkle with a few thyme leaves.

Marinated Lemon Salad

You should use large, sweet lemons for this salad. And whilst I like this on its own as a side salad, you can also use it as a base, or as a textured dressing – try tossing the whole lot with white beans or lentils, or perhaps with a big pile of rocket. Or eat with a fresh, mild curd cheese.

Cut the pith and skin off 3–4 lemons (see page 15), depending on size, then slice into rounds, flicking out the pips as you go. Arrange over a plate and sprinkle with a few sprigs of rosemary. Season with salt then drizzle over some olive oil. Leave to stand at room temperature for a few hours if possible. Lightly toast 2 tbsp flaked almonds in a frying pan. Sprinkle these over the lemons and serve.

Grapefruit, Tomato and Mint Salad, with a Pomegranate Molasses Dressing

Another citrus/tomato combination I love. This is good with buttery couscous and flaked almonds.

Segment 2 grapefruit (see page 15). Cut 200g/7oz cherry tomatoes in half. Pare a cucumber into thin ribbons with a swivel peeler. Mix them all in a bowl with 1 quantity Lime-Pickled Red Onions (see page 26). For the dressing, whisk together 2 tbsp olive oil with 1 tbsp lemon juice, 1 tbsp pomegranate molasses, and a pinch each of ground cinnamon and ground cardamom. Season with salt and pepper. Pour the dressing over the vegetables and lightly toss. Serve with a few parsley and mint leaves.

Carrot, Orange and Orange Blossom Salad

This is a very refreshing salad with a satisfying crunch. It could be described as a Moroccan-inspired coleslaw and will work well on the side with anything spiced.

Peel and julienne around 400g/14oz carrots – they need to be a shape and size similar to matchsticks. Add 50g/⅓ cup pistachio nibs (pistachios that have been skinned and cut into slivers) or crush or chop some regular pistachios. Mix 2 tbsp olive oil with 2 tsp lemon juice and the juice of 1 orange. Add a few drops of orange blossom water, then season and whisk until well combined. Pour over the carrots and pistachios, then mix. Garnish with some freshly chopped parsley or mint.

Courgette, Parmesan and Lemon Salad

I based this on one of my favourite salads from London's Polpo restaurant. The trick is to use courgettes (zucchini) that are young and small.

Thinly slice around 400g/14oz courgettes into rounds. Put in a bowl, then add 1 crushed garlic clove, the finely grated zest of 1 lemon, 2 tbsp olive oil and the juice of ½ lemon. Season with salt and pepper, then stir everything through. Sprinkle over around 30g/scant ½ cup freshly grated Parmesan and stir again. Garnish with plenty of basil leaves.

Jerusalem Artichoke and Preserved Orange

I had no idea Jerusalem artichokes could be eaten raw until I was once served a salad of them by Danish cook Trine Hahnemann. They are a revelation: sweet and crisp – a bit like jicama but slightly denser in texture.

Add the juice of ½ lemon to a bowl of ice-cold water. Peel about 8 medium artichokes then slice them in very thin rounds, dropping them into the acidulated water as you go. When you are ready to serve, drain them thoroughly and arrange over a plate. Julienne 1 tbsp preserved Seville orange zest (see page 21) and mix with 2 tsp of some of the liquor from the preserved orange, then thin with 2 tbsp fresh orange juice. Drizzle over the artichokes, followed by a drizzle of olive oil. This looks beautifully pure as it is, but would also be good with a light sprinkling of micro coriander (cilantro).

Main Courses

You can do a lot of mixing and matching with the recipes throughout this section. Many of them rely on classic citrus sauces such as gremolata, harissa and salsas, or on those that typically don't always contain citrus but work extremely well with the addition, such as pesto. Most of these can be made in larger quantities for quick meals with grilled or roasted meats, fish and vegetables.

Play with flavour combinations too. Preserved orange or lime tastes very different to preserved lemon, but can be used in casseroles or sauces in the same way. A pasta sauce traditionally made with lemon and basil, is wonderful, but so, too, is the combination of lime and tarragon. I give suggestions throughout but please don't be limited by these. One rule I do follow is regarding peel and zest. The fruits with sour juice – lemon, lime, sour orange – tend to have a zest that can be used unadulterated in savoury dishes without blanching. Grapefruit is the exception here – I find a small amount of microplaned zest is fine, but any more and I need to blanch it. The zest from those with a sweeter juice – oranges and the smaller oranges bred for sweetness, such as clementines – tends to give a bitter note if not blanched first. So be careful when adding whole pieces of peel or zest to casseroles, sauces and rice dishes.

Lime-Marinated Fish with a Lime, Garlic and Basil Sauce

Serves 4

4 fillets of a firm fish, such as red
  snapper or sea bass, skinned

1 tbsp olive oil

15g/1 tbsp butter

Sea salt and freshly ground black
  pepper

For the marinade

Finely grated zest and juice of 2 limes

3 garlic cloves, crushed

½ Scotch bonnet chilli, very finely
  chopped

50ml/3½ tbsp white wine

For the sauce

250ml/generous 1 cup crème fraîche

4 garlic cloves, sliced

Finely grated zest of 1 lime

A pinch of sugar (optional)

A squeeze of lime juice (optional)

1 egg yolk

A bunch of basil leaves

This is a recipe I developed years ago when in the French West Indies. When I first started exploring Caribbean food I was amazed at the overlap with flavours that we think of as Mediterranean, such as basil. The fish has a deeply savoury quality that is mellowed out by the creamy lime and basil-sweetened sauce.

Put the fish fillets in a bowl and season with salt and pepper. For the marinade, mix the lime zest and juice with the garlic, chilli and wine. Pour this over the fish fillets and leave to marinate for at least an hour in the refrigerator.

To make the sauce, put the crème fraîche in a saucepan with the garlic. Heat gently, just to loosen the crème fraîche, without allowing it to boil. Remove from the heat and leave to infuse for around 30 minutes. Strain into a clean saucepan, then whisk in the lime zest. Season with salt and taste – you might find it needs a pinch of sugar and a squeeze of lime.

To cook the fish, heat the olive oil and butter in a frying pan large enough to hold the fillets, with space for manoeuvre. When the butter starts to foam, remove the fish from the marinade and lightly pat dry with kitchen paper. Add to the pan and fry for 3–4 minutes until the underside is crisp and will easily come away from the base of the frying pan – the flesh should also be opaque until halfway up the side of the fillet. Flip over and continue to cook for a further 2–3 minutes.

Set aside to rest while you whisk the egg yolk into the sauce over a very gentle heat. Stir in the basil and serve the fillets with the sauce spooned over at the table.

Whole Baked Fish
with Lemon and Ouzo

Serves 4

1kg/2lb 3oz new potatoes, scrubbed

2 tbsp olive oil, plus extra for the fish and capers

30g/2 tbsp butter

Finely grated zest and juice of 1 lemon, plus 1 lemon, sliced

1 head of garlic, broken up into cloves, left unpeeled

1 large sea bass or similar (around 1kg/2lb 3oz) or 2 smaller, cleaned and descaled

A few sprigs of thyme and or/lemon thyme and dill

100ml/7 tbsp white wine

50ml/3½ tbsp ouzo or other anise-based spirit

2 tbsp capers

Sea salt and freshly ground black pepper

For the lemon and ouzo sauce

2 egg yolks

1 tsp Dijon mustard

200ml/generous ¾ cup neutral-tasting oil, such as sunflower or groundnut

50ml/3½ tbsp Greek yogurt

2 tbsp ouzo or similar anise-based spirit

Juice of ½ lemon

A pinch of sugar (optional)

1 tbsp finely chopped dill

½ tsp fennel seeds, finely crushed (optional)

This is one of the easiest ways to cook fish. It is also a complete, one-pot dish, although you can bake the fish separately, wrapped in foil, if you prefer. I normally make this with lemon, but it is also good with fragrant mandarins, which work well with aniseedy ouzo.

Preheat the oven to 200°C/400°F/Gas mark 6.

Boil the potatoes for 10 minutes in plenty of salted water until just tender. Run under cold water until cool enough to handle. Squash in your hands so they break roughly in half, then put in a roasting tin.

Heat the olive oil and the butter together until the butter has melted then add the lemon zest and juice. Pour all but a tablespoon of this mixture over the potatoes and season with salt and pepper. Add the garlic cloves, reserving a couple for the fish. Roast in the oven for 30 minutes.

Cut a few slits into the fish on both sides. Peel and finely slice the reserved garlic and stuff some into the slits along with a few herb sprigs. Put the lemon slices, more herbs and a few more slices of garlic in the cavity of the fish.

Put the fish on top of the potatoes, then drizzle over the reserved tablespoon of lemony butter and a little more olive oil. Mix the wine and ouzo together and pour this over the fish and potatoes. Roast in the oven for a further 25–30 minutes until the fish is just cooked through.

Meanwhile, make the sauce. Put the egg yolks and mustard in a bowl with a pinch of salt. Start drizzling in the oil, very gradually, whisking with a balloon whisk until it emulsifies and starts to thicken. At this point you can speed up the drizzling a little. When you have incorporated all the oil, whisk in the yogurt, ouzo and lemon juice. Season with salt, then taste – you may need a little more, along with a pinch of sugar to balance out the flavours. Stir in the dill and the fennel seeds, if using.

For the caper garnish, heat a tablespoon of olive oil in a frying pan. When very hot, add the capers – they will splutter for a few moments. When it subsides, remove from the heat. Pour over the fish and serve immediately.

Harissa Mackerel with Orange-Scented Couscous

Serves 4

8 large mackerel fillets

A little olive oil

For the harissa

1 tsp cumin seeds

½ tsp coriander seeds

½ tsp caraway seeds

½ tsp black peppercorns

4 fat green chillies, preferably jalapeño

1 tbsp preserved lemon peel, finely chopped (see page 21)

Finely grated zest and juice of ½ lemon

1 garlic clove, finely chopped

1 slice of fresh root ginger, peeled and finely chopped

25g/1½ cups fresh parsley

10g/¾ cup fresh coriander (cilantro) leaves

10g/¾ cup fresh lemon verbena or lemon balm (or mint, at a pinch)

2 tbsp olive oil

Cayenne, to taste (optional)

Sea salt and black pepper

For the couscous

A strip of blanched, dried orange zest (see page 18)

150g/¾ cup wholegrain couscous

50g/⅓ cup dates, finely chopped

Juice of 1 orange

½ tsp orange blossom water

15g/1 tbsp butter

50g/⅓ cup pistachio nibs (skinned and slivered kernels)

A small bunch of parsley, finely chopped

What is it about a plump, oily fish that lends itself so perfectly to heat and spice? The results are always immensely satisfying on the palate. If you like, rather than serve the remaining harissa on the side, you can stir it through some yogurt, just to lessen the intensity. You can make this with sardines in place of the mackerel; just use 16 fillets instead of 8.

To make the harissa, lightly toast the cumin, coriander and caraway seeds and peppercorns in a dry frying pan until fragrant, then cool and grind to a powder. Add the chillies to the same pan and cook until the skin starts to blister on all sides. Remove, then deseed when cool enough to handle, and roughly chop.

Put the spices, chilli and all the remaining ingredients except the seasoning into a food processor and pulse, scraping down regularly, until you have a coarse paste. Season with salt and pepper then taste – you may want to add more heat; if so add in some cayenne.

Use half the harissa to marinate the mackerel: score the mackerel 3–4 times across the skin (this helps it keep its shape when cooked), then put into a bowl and rub the harissa over it. Leave for 30 minutes.

Preheat the grill to its highest setting. Put the mackerel fillets on a baking tray, skin side up. Drizzle over a little olive oil and sprinkle with salt, then grill for 5 minutes until the skin is crisp and the flesh is just cooked through.

To make the couscous, finely chop or blitz the dried orange zest. Put it in a bowl with the couscous and dates and a good pinch of salt. Measure the orange juice and top it up with hot, but not boiling, water to 200ml/¾ cup plus 1 tablespoon. Add the orange blossom water, then pour over the couscous and dates. Add the butter and leave to stand until all the liquid is absorbed and the couscous fluffs up well with a fork. Stir through the pistachios and parsley.

Serve the mackerel fillets with the remaining harissa and the couscous on the side.

Salmon Fillets with Mandarin and Ginger

Serves 4

4 salmon fillets, skinned

Finely grated zest and juice of 3 mandarins

Finely grated zest and juice of 1 lemon

1 tsp ground cardamom

3cm/1½-in piece of fresh root ginger, peeled and grated

2 tbsp olive oil

2 onions, finely sliced

3 garlic cloves, finely chopped

1 tbsp dark soy sauce

1 tbsp rice vinegar

1 tbsp mirin

250g/1½ cups cooked wild, red or black rice (125g/¾ cup raw)

200g/1 cup cooked puy lentils (80g/ scant ⅓ cup raw)

1 large head of broccoli, separated into florets and cooked to al dente

Sea salt and finely ground white pepper

Sesame seeds, to serve

This is a storecupboard dish. I've made similar with the same citrus using pomegranate molasses in place of the soy sauce, rice vinegar and mirin, and used mung beans in place of the puy lentils. In other words, it is very adaptable; you can vary the flavours to suit your tastes.

Rub the salmon fillets with the mandarin and lemon zest, the cardamom and the ginger. Sprinkle over a little salt and some finely ground white pepper and put aside for a few minutes.

Heat the oil in a large frying pan. Add the onions and sauté for several minutes until soft and translucent. Add the garlic and cook for a further couple of minutes. Push everything to one side, then add the salmon fillets. Cook for 4 minutes on one side, then turn over. Pour over the mandarin and lemon juices along with the soy sauce, rice vinegar and mirin. Simmer for 2 minutes, then turn the salmon over again. When it is cooked to your liking, remove and keep warm. Stir the onion and garlic into the sauce and cook until syrupy.

Serve the salmon with the rice, beans or lentils and broccoli, with the sauce spooned over and a few sesame seeds sprinkled over.

Spiced Sea Bass with Citrus Butter Sauce

Serves 4

4 sea bass fillets, skin on

1 tbsp olive oil

30g/2 tbsp butter

2 garlic cloves, finely chopped

Finely grated zest and juice of
  2 lemons

Juice of 1 large orange

100ml/7 tbsp water

Sea salt and freshly ground black
  pepper

For the rub

1 tsp flaky sea salt, pounded

½ tsp ground cardamom

¼ tsp ground cinnamon

¼ tsp ground ginger

¼ tsp ground white pepper

¼ tsp garlic powder

¼ tsp ground turmeric

To serve

350g/12oz spring greens, very
  finely shredded

350g/2½ cups cooked chickpeas
  (garbanzo beans)

The spicing here is fragrant rather than hot and has a vaguely Middle Eastern feel to it, so you could simply serve it with rice or couscous instead of the chickpeas and greens if you prefer.

Blot the sea bass fillets and lie skin-side down on kitchen paper. Combine all the rub ingredients and sprinkle evenly over the fillets. Press lightly.

Before you start frying the fish, cook the spring greens. Wash thoroughly, then put in a large lidded saucepan without shaking off too much water. Cover and heat gently until the greens have wilted down and are just al dente – they should be a fresh, bright green.

Heat the olive oil in a large frying pan. When hot, add the sea bass fillets, skin side down, and fry for a couple of minutes. Flip over and cook for a further 30 seconds. Remove from the frying pan and keep warm.

Add the butter, garlic, lemon zest and juice and orange juice to the pan. Turn up the heat and let the mixture bubble until you have a glossy, syrupy sauce. Pour into a jug.

Deglaze the pan with the water. Add the chickpeas and spring greens and stir to pick up any flavour residue. Season with salt and pepper.

Serve the fish with the chickpeas and greens, and the sauce spooned over.

Fish Tacos

Serves 4

4 firm, thick white fish fillets, skinned and cut in half

Olive oil

Sea salt and freshly ground black pepper

For the marinade

2 tbsp olive oil

Finely grated zest and juice of 1 lime

Finely grated zest and juice of 1 mandarin (optional)

1 tsp ground cumin

½ tsp chilli powder

1 tsp dried oregano

1 tsp garlic powder

1 tsp salt

For the tomatillo, grapefruit and chilli salsa

4 tomatillos (or green tomatoes, or failing that, just use red), diced

½ red onion, diced, or the same amount of Lime-Pickled Red Onions (see page 26)

1 garlic clove, finely chopped

1 large pink or red grapefruit, segmented (see page 15) and diced

1 red chilli, finely chopped

A pinch of ground cumin

Juice of 1 lime

1 tsp red wine vinegar

2 tbsp chopped coriander (cilantro)

This looks like a lot of work, but really it takes minutes to make the salsas while the fish gets a brief marinating. I prefer to make my own tortillas, and usually use a heavy frying pan to squash them flat as I don't have a tortilla press, but you don't have to do this yourself – it is possible to buy very good ones.

You can experiment with the flavours in the salsa – I like something quite tart against savoury fish and sweet avocado, so in place of grapefruit I might use blood orange or physalis.

First prepare the fish. In a bowl, whisk together the marinade ingredients, pour over the fish fillets and leave to marinate for at least an hour.

Meanwhile, make the salsas. Mix the ingredients for each in 2 separate bowls and season well with salt and pepper. Leave to stand – these are best at room temperature. (You can purée the avocado if you like a crema – I prefer it chunky.)

Heat a frying pan until very hot, then add a little olive oil. Add the fish fillets and cook until they are almost completely done (i.e. the flesh will be turning opaque up the sides), then flip for another minute. Remove from the pan.

Pile the fillets onto the tortillas and top with shredded lettuce and the salsas.

ingredients and method continue overleaf...

continued...

For the avocado salsa

1 large avocado, diced

Finely grated zest and juice of 1 lime

2 tbsp coconut cream

2 tbsp chopped coriander (cilantro)

To serve

Fresh corn tortillas (see right,
  or use shop bought)

Shredded lettuce

250g/2½ cups masa harina

330ml/1¼ cups plus 3 tbsp
  just-boiled water

Corn Tortillas

Put the masa harina in a bowl and pour in the water. Start mixing with a spoon, then when it starts to come together, turn out onto a work surface and knead until the dough is smooth. Make sure it isn't too dry – if it looks as though cracks are appearing or may appear, incorporate a little more hot water by wetting your hands and continuing to knead. Divide the mixture into 8 pieces and roll each piece into a ball.

If you own a tortilla press, place plastic wrap over the bottom, place a ball of dough in the centre of the press, then cover with more plastic wrap. Press down as firmly as you can then lift up. Carefully peel away the top layer of plastic wrap and lift off the second, taking the tortilla with it – you should have a tortilla around 15cm/6-in in diameter. Don't worry if it is slightly rough around the edges, this just makes them look more rustic. If you don't have a tortilla press, use a heavy-based saucepan or frying pan instead, making sure it is placed centrally over the dough before you press down. Keep the uncooked tortillas to one side, divided by layers of plastic wrap, until you are ready to cook them.

To cook the tortillas, heat a heavy-based frying pan or griddle pan to medium–hot. Cook each tortilla for a minimum of 15 seconds on one side then try to lift off – if it doesn't come cleanly away, you need to cook it for slightly longer. Flip over and cook for a further 30 seconds, and again, don't remove until it will come cleanly away. Flip one last time and cook for another 15 seconds. Keep warm while you make the remaining tortillas.

Lamb Meatballs with Broad Beans, Chard and Preserved Lemon

Serves 4

For the meatballs

500g/1lb 2oz minced lamb

50g/2½ tbsp pine nuts, lightly toasted

50g/⅔ cup fine breadcrumbs

1 onion, finely chopped

2 garlic cloves, finely chopped

½ tsp ground allspice

A pinch of ground cinnamon

½ tsp dried mint

1 egg

50ml/3½ tbsp cream or thick yogurt

Finely grated zest and juice of 1 lemon

For the meatball sauce

1 tbsp olive oil

1 onion, finely chopped

A large bunch of chard, stems and
  leaves separated and shredded

Finely grated zest and juice of 1 lemon

2 garlic cloves, finely chopped

½ tsp ground allspice

300ml/1¼ cups chicken stock

250g/2 cups shelled broad beans
  (fava beans), skinned if you like

A small bunch of parsley, finely chopped

A small bunch of dill, finely chopped

A small bunch of mint, finely chopped

For the yogurt sauce

200ml/generous ¾ cup Greek yogurt

1 preserved lemon, or 1 tbsp Cheat's
  Preserved Lemon (see page 22), chopped

1 tsp sumac

1 tsp dried mint

I do love dishes that combine both fresh and preserved citrus. Here fresh lemon bestows on the meatballs and greens both depth of flavour and fragrance, whilst the preserved lemon and sumac work to provide the sour notes.

First make the meatballs. Preheat the oven to 200°C/400°F/Gas mark 6. Put all the ingredients into a bowl, with salt and pepper to taste, and mix thoroughly. Test a small piece of mixture for seasoning by frying in a little oil in a small frying pan, and adjusting the seasoning accordingly. Form the mixture into golf ball-sized pieces, place on a baking tray and bake for around 10–12 minutes.

Meanwhile, make the sauce. Heat the oil in a large flameproof casserole or wide, deep sided frying pan. Add the onion and chard stems with a squeeze of the lemon juice and sauté until softened. Add the lemon zest, garlic and allspice and cook for a couple more minutes. Pour in the stock and bring to the boil. Add the broad beans (fava beans), chard leaves and two thirds of the chopped herbs. Simmer for 4–5 minutes until the vegetables are tender, then add the baked meatballs and simmer for another few minutes just to meld the flavours. Add the remaining lemon juice to taste and sprinkle with the reserved herbs.

Stir the yogurt sauce ingredients together. Season with salt and pepper. Serve the meatballs with the vegetables and the yogurt sauce on the side.

Greek-Style Lamb Chops with Feta and Celeriac Mash

Serves 4

Around 12 lamb chops (more if you
are all very hungry), at least 2cm/
¾-in thick

Finely grated zest and juice of 2 lemons

1 tbsp dried mountain herbs
(e.g. a mixture of oregano, thyme, sage,
rosemary)

1 tbsp olive oil

1 garlic clove, finely chopped (optional)

Sea salt

For the mash

4 medium potatoes, peeled and cut
into small chunks

½ large celeriac, peeled and cut into
small chunks

15g/1 tbsp butter, plus extra for the
dish and top

100g/3½oz feta, broken into chunks

To garnish (optional)

1 tbsp olive oil

1 tbsp capers

1 lemon, segmented (see page 15)
and diced

Variation

**I once – unaccountably – ran out
of lemons, so I used a tablespoon
of ground, dried lemon myrtle with
a little Dijon mustard and orange
juice in their place, and just added
a pinch of oregano, no other herbs.
It worked beautifully.**

**One of my favourite things about going to visit my
parents in Greece is that I get to drive up the mountains
to a particular taverna, and gorge on their charcoal-
grilled lamb chops. The mountain herbs vary from visit
to visit, but the flavour is always superb.**

**You can't really beat the taste of these cooked over fire,
but at a pinch, griddle or grill them instead.**

Put the lamb chops in a non-reactive container. Sprinkle
with salt and rub it into the flesh lightly. Mix the lemon
zest and juice with the herbs, olive oil and garlic, if using,
and rub this over the flesh too. Leave to marinate for a
good couple of hours, overnight (refrigerated) if you are
able to.

To make the mash, preheat the oven to 200°C/400°F/
Gas mark 6. Put the potatoes and celeriac into a saucepan
and cover with water. Add salt, bring to the boil, then
turn down and simmer until tender. Drain, add the butter
and mash together. Butter an ovenproof dish and pile the
mash into it. Push the feta into the top, leaving it slightly
exposed (or at least flush with the mash), then dot with a
little more butter. Bake in the oven for around 20 minutes
until the feta is soft and lightly browned in patches.

When you are ready to cook the chops, prepare your
barbecue. If you have any dried lemon peel lying around,
soak for a little while in water. When the coals are white,
add the lemon peel – it will add smoke and aroma.
Arrange the lamb chops around the side (they need
indirect heat initially) and cook for around 3 minutes on
each side, basting with any dregs of marinade, then move
to the centre of the grill to get a decent charring. Leave for
at least 5 minutes to rest before eating.

For the optional garnish, heat the olive oil in a small pan
and when it is very hot, throw in the capers and lemon.
Toss for a few seconds – they should sizzle and brown
immediately, so be careful, it might spit at you. Pour this
over the mash when it comes out of the oven.

Lamb or Goat with Sour Orange, Chilli and Coriander

Serves 4

A large bunch of coriander (cilantro)

2–3 hot red chillies, deseeded if you like

1 head of garlic, cloves separated and peeled

2 tbsp olive oil

1 large onion, finely sliced

1kg/2lb 3oz lamb, mutton or goat shoulder, cut into large chunks and trimmed of fat

250ml/generous 1 cup sour orange juice (or 150ml/10 tbsp orange juice and 100ml/7 tbsp lime juice)

1kg/2lb 3oz new or salad potatoes, washed and sliced

500g/3 cups petit pois

Sea salt and freshly ground black pepper

I am repeating myself with this recipe as it is one of my favourite recipes from my pressure cooker book – but the combination of heat, citrus and sweetness from the lamb and peas is so wonderful I couldn't not replicate it here, albeit with conventional instructions. The original recipe is based on a Peruvian dish recorded by Elisabeth Lambert Ortiz.

Set aside a third of the coriander (cilantro), then purée the rest in a small food processor with the chillies, garlic and 1 tablespoon of the olive oil. If it proves resistant, add a little water.

Heat the remaining oil in a large flameproof casserole. Add the onion and sauté for a few minutes on a medium heat until starting to soften. Add the coriander paste and continue to cook, stirring, until it starts to brown a little. Add the meat. Cook for several minutes on a high heat, turning over regularly until the meat looks lightly browned and is completely coated in the paste. Season with salt and pepper.

Pour over the citrus juices and add just enough water to cover the lamb. Bring to the boil then turn down the heat, cover and simmer gently for about 1½ hours. Add the potatoes and peas and continue to cook, covered, until the potatoes are completely tender.

Finely chop the remaining coriander and stir it into the casserole just before serving.

Tonkatsu with Yuzu Coleslaw and Ponzu

Serves 4

For the pork

8 pork medallions or steaks, trimmed of fat

2 tbsp plain (all-purpose) flour

2 eggs, beaten

100g/2⅓ cups panko breadcrumbs

30g/2 tbsp butter, melted, or olive oil

Sea salt and black pepper

For the coleslaw

½ small green (pointed) cabbage

1 carrot, peeled and julienned

4 spring onions (scallions), finely chopped

½ tsp salt

½ tsp caster (superfine) sugar

2 tsp white wine vinegar

1 crisp apple, peeled and grated

1 tbsp mayonnaise

1 tbsp crème fraîche

1 tbsp yuzu juice, or more to taste

A dash of dark soy sauce

½ tsp powdered yuzu zest (optional)

1 tbsp sesame seeds

For the ponzu

3 tbsp dark soy sauce

1 tbsp mirin

1 tbsp rice vinegar

½ tsp sugar

1 thin slice of fresh root ginger, peeled and finely chopped

Juice of 1 mandarin

2 tbsp yuzu juice

1 tsp powdered yuzu zest

Tonkatsu is the Japanese version of schnitzel, made with panko crumbs. You could serve it as such with lots of freshly squeezed lemon and it would still be a wonderful meal. But this is even better. Usually just juice is used in ponzu, but I do like to ramp up the flavour of the yuzu by adding powdered zest as well – that is where most of the fragrance is to be found.

First make the coleslaw. Shred the cabbage as finely as you can, then put in a colander with the carrot and spring onions (scallions). Sprinkle over the salt, sugar and vinegar, then leave to stand over a bowl or in the sink for an hour – this will have the effect of ridding the vegetables of any excess water and will prevent it from diluting the dressing later. Transfer the vegetables to a bowl and add the apple. Whisk together the mayonnaise, crème fraîche, yuzu juice, soy and powdered zest, if using. Pour over the vegetables and mix thoroughly. Sprinkle over the sesame seeds.

To make the tonkatsu, preheat the oven to 200°C/400°F/ Gas mark 6. Put the pork between sheets of plastic wrap and bash with a mallet or rolling pin until they are as thin as you can get without them breaking up. Put the flour on a plate and season with salt and pepper. Put the beaten eggs into a small bowl and the breadcrumbs on a separate plate. Dust each escalope with the seasoned flour, then pat off any excess before dropping into the egg wash and then the breadcrumbs. Arrange on a baking tray. Drizzle over the melted butter or oil and bake in the oven for around 10–12 minutes, by which point the pork should be cooked through and the breadcrumbs lightly browned.

To make the ponzu, put the soy sauce, mirin, rice vinegar, sugar, ginger, mandarin juice and lime juice in a small saucepan. Simmer, stirring, until the sugar has dissolved, then immediately remove from the heat. Whisk in the yuzu juice and zest and strain into a small dipping sauce bowl.

Serve the pork with the coleslaw on the side and the ponzu for dipping.

Szechuan Peppercorn and Orange Beef

Serves 4

1 large piece of onglet, split lengthways along its central vein (a butcher will do this for you)

1 tsp olive oil, plus extra for rubbing

15g/1 tbsp butter

1 shallot, finely chopped

1 garlic clove, finely chopped

2cm/¾-in piece of fresh root ginger, peeled and finely chopped

2–3 red chillies, sliced

1 tsp Szechuan peppercorns, lightly crushed

Juice of 1 orange

1 tbsp rice wine vinegar

1 tbsp light soy sauce

For the celeriac fries

¼ celeriac, julienned

1 tbsp olive oil

For the rub

2 tbsp Szechuan peppercorns

1 tsp coriander seeds

1 tsp garlic powder

½ tsp black peppercorns

2 tsp dried orange or mandarin zest

To garnish

2 oranges, peel and membrane cut away (see page 15) and sliced into rounds

½ cucumber, peeled, halved lengthways, deseeded and cut on the diagonal into crescents

4 spring onions (scallions), halved lengthways and cut into slivers

A handful of basil, shredded

Hot and sour from orange zest, Szechuan peppercorns and chilli, with a sweet, cooling side salad, this makes for a perfectly balanced meal, taste-wise. I am usually happy to leave this as is, but you could serve it over noodles or rice if you wanted to.

For the celeriac fries, preheat the oven to 200°C/400°F/ Gas mark 6. Toss the celeriac in the olive oil and plenty of sea salt. Arrange over a baking tray and roast for 15–20 minutes, stirring regularly, until matchstick thin and crisp. Drain on kitchen paper.

Meanwhile, to make the rub, toast the spices in a dry frying pan until they smell aromatic. Remove and transfer to a plate to cool, then grind in a pestle and mortar with ½ teaspoon of salt and the dried zest. Pat dry the onglet, then rub over with olive oil. Sprinkle over a tablespoon of the rub, patting it in as much as you can. Set aside for a few minutes.

Heat a frying pan (preferably not non-stick) until it's too hot to hold your hand over, and add the teaspoon of olive oil. Sear the steak on all sides, making sure you allow a good crust to develop before you turn it. Remove from the pan and leave to rest for at least 10 minutes.

Turn down the heat and add the butter to the pan – it should foam immediately. Add the shallot and sauté for a few minutes to soften, then add the garlic, ginger, chillies and Szechuan peppercorns. Cook for a further minute, then pour in the orange juice, the rice wine vinegar and the soy sauce. Simmer until the mixture is syrupy, then pour in any juices from the resting steak. Cut the steak into slices. Put on a platter and spoon over the sauce.

For the salad garnish, put the orange and cucumber in a bowl with any juice squeezed from the discarded orange peel. Season with salt and add the spring onions (scallions) and shredded basil.

Serve the celeriac fries over the beef with the salad on the side.

Beef Casserole with Orange and Juniper

Serves 4

1kg/2lb 3oz beef (ox cheek, shin,
  or skirt), cut into large pieces

2 tbsp plain (all-purpose) flour

1 tsp mustard powder

2 tbsp neutral-tasting oil, such as
  sunflower or groundnut

15g/1 tbsp butter

1 onion, finely diced

1 carrot, finely diced

2 celery sticks, finely diced

1 tsp juniper berries

2 large strips of pared orange zest,
  blanched twice (or dried if you have it)

3 garlic cloves, finely chopped

A sprig of thyme

2 bay leaves

Juice of 2 oranges

1 bottle of red wine

Sea salt and freshly ground black
  pepper

**You do not have to stick with beef in this recipe –
venison or a fatty cut of pork such as pig cheeks
will also love this treatment. And if you are looking
for a good side dish to serve with this, please
consider trying the Caramelized Potatoes with Orange
on page 134 – they complement the earthy juniper
perfectly, as well as bringing out the subtle flavours of
orange in the casserole.**

Trim off any large pieces of fat from the beef, then pat it
dry if necessary and put in a large bowl. Mix the flour and
mustard powder with some salt and pepper, tip the lot
over the beef then toss lightly to coat.

Heat 1 tablespoon of the oil in a large frying pan. Sear the
beef on all sides, then remove.

In a flameproof casserole, heat the remaining oil and the
butter. Add the onion, carrot and celery, then sauté on a
medium heat until the vegetables have started to take on
a bit of colour. Add the juniper and pared orange strips,
along with the garlic, thyme and bay. Stir for a minute,
then add the seared beef.

Pour over the orange juice and let it reduce almost to
a syrup, then pour over the red wine. Bring to the boil,
then turn down the heat to its lowest setting, cover and
cook for at least a couple of hours, until the beef is very
tender. Remove the lid and continue to simmer to reduce
the sauce, then serve with either a large pile of mashed
potatoes or the Caramelized Potatoes with Orange.

Beef Short Ribs
with Lemongrass and Lime

Serves 4

1 tbsp coconut oil

6 large, meaty short ribs

6 shallots, roughly chopped

5cm/2-in piece of fresh root ginger, peeled and chopped

1 head of garlic, cloves peeled and chopped

4 lemongrass stalks, peeled, white part sliced

A small bunch of coriander (cilantro), separated into stems and leaves

Finely grated zest and juice of 1 lime

A pinch of ground cinnamon

A pinch of ground cloves

2 tbsp tomato paste

1 tbsp tamarind paste

300ml/1¼ cups beef stock

400ml/generous 1½ cups coconut milk

50ml/3½ tbsp fish sauce (or light soy sauce)

1 tbsp palm sugar (or soft light brown sugar)

3 star anise

2 lime leaves, shredded (optional)

Sea salt and freshly ground black pepper

To serve

2 carrots, julienned

1 green papaya, peeled and julienned

Juice of ½ lime

1 tbsp fish sauce

A few coriander (cilantro) leaves

This dish is quite lengthy in method time if not preparation, purely because the cooking liquor needs to rest so that the fat from the short ribs can be removed. However, the benefit of this is that it does taste better on the second day, and the liquor makes a good soup base, so it is almost two meals in one. Any leftovers are good shredded or pulled – eat over rice, with noodles, mix with beansprouts and shredded carrot and put in spring rolls, or go fusion and serve as tacos.

Heat a teaspoon of the coconut oil in a large, heavy-based frying pan, then add the short ribs and fry on all sides until very well seared and a rich dark brown. Do not stint on this step; it will take up to 10 minutes to do properly.

Put the shallots, ginger, garlic, lemongrass, coriander (cilantro) stems, lime zest and juice into a small food processor with a splash of water and blitz – you want a fairly smooth texture. Heat the remaining coconut oil in a large flameproof casserole. Add the freshly made paste and fry on a medium heat for several minutes until very aromatic and starting to brown, then add the spices, tomato paste and tamarind paste. Cook, stirring constantly, for a couple more minutes. Add the short ribs and turn to coat in the paste, then pour over the stock, coconut milk and fish or soy sauce. Add the sugar, star anise and lime leaves, if using. Bring to the boil and season with salt and pepper. Turn down, cover and cook for around 1½–2 hours, until the short ribs are tender and threatening to detach themselves from the bone.

Remove the short ribs to a plate, then pour the cooking liquor into a refrigerator-friendly container. When it is cool, chill until you can easily scrape off the fat that will collect at the top. At this point you can reheat the liquor and ribs together, reducing the liquid a little.

To make the salad, sprinkle the carrots and papaya with salt and leave to stand for 30 minutes, then rinse and mix with the lime juice and fish sauce. Add the coriander leaves and serve the salad with the ribs.

Pork and Grapefruit or Pomelo Stir Fry

Serves 4

1 tbsp groundnut oil (or other neutral-tasting oil)

10g/⅓oz fresh root ginger, peeled and finely chopped

A bunch of spring onions (scallions), whites and greens separated, sliced

2 garlic cloves, sliced

2 red chillies, sliced

1 red (bell) pepper, cut into strips

75g/2½oz pomelo pith, prepared in advance as below (omit if using grapefruit)

400g/14oz pork tenderloin, cut into strips

100ml/7 tbsp coconut milk

1 tbsp fish sauce

A squeeze of lime juice (optional)

30g/1oz fresh coconut flesh, cut into thin slivers and lightly toasted

1 grapefruit or pomelo, segmented (see page 15)

A handful of Thai basil

Sea salt and freshly ground black pepper

Steamed jasmine rice or noodles, to serve

This recipe contains an optional addition of pomelo pith, which needs some fairly intense boiling before you can use it. It isn't essential, but if you are using pomelo it is worth trying the pith at least once, as it adds an extra dimension to both the flavour and texture of the stir fry.

Heat the oil in a large wok. When it is hot – the air above it should be shimmering – add the ginger, spring onion (scallion) whites, garlic, chillies, red (bell) pepper and pomelo pith, if using pomelo not grapefruit. Fry for 2–3 minutes, stirring constantly, then add the pork. Season with salt and pepper.

Stir fry for another minute or two then, still on a high heat, add the coconut milk and fish sauce. Cook for 3–4 minutes until the sauce has reduced a little, then taste and squeeze in some lime juice if you think it needs it. Remove from the heat and add the toasted coconut, grapefruit or pomelo segments and the Thai basil. Sprinkle with the spring onion (scallion) greens and serve immediately with jasmine rice or some noodles, and perhaps some oriental greens on the side.

To prepare the pomelo pith

Make sure none of the zest is still attached (use this for something else) and cut the pith into thick slices. Soak in water for 24 hours, changing the water several times, then boil for 10 minutes or until completely transparent. Drain thoroughly.

Totally Tropical Ham with Glazed Grapefruit and Pineapple, and Sweetcorn Fritters

Serves 4, with leftovers

1 smoked ham or gammon (around 2.5–3kg/5½–6½ lb)

1.5 litres/generous 6 cups Ting or Lilt

500ml/generous 2 cups lager or similar light beer

1 tsp allspice berries, lightly crushed

1 small slice of Scotch bonnet chilli

A few pieces of mace

2 onions, quartered

A few garlic cloves

2 cloves

A few slices of fresh root ginger

2 bay leaves

1 large sprig of woody thyme

For the garnish

1 tbsp rum

1 tbsp runny honey

4 thick slices of pineapple

4 fat slices of grapefruit, taken from the middle of 2 grapefruit

Ah, that grapefruit/pineapple combo, so beloved by people in the UK until – when? When did we stop drinking Lilt? It is still available but has somehow slipped out of the national consciousness. I use it here, or, when possible, use Ting instead. Ting is a grapefruit-flavoured soft drink from the Caribbean which can be found in some supermarkets and Caribbean grocery stores. I love it – it's not as sweet as a lot of soft drinks and is excellent in a shandy. The ham/fizzy drink combo isn't unprecedented. People (including, of course, Nigella Lawson) have been cooking ham in cola for years. I like the close, dense texture it produces for the ham, and the cooking liquor is a very good base for a black bean soup.

If frying sweetcorn fritters as well as grilling fruit is a bit of a stretch, you can always use the same ingredients and make a salsa instead. Toast the sweetcorn in a pan until lightly charred, then add the rest of the vegetables and seasonings and a dash of soy sauce, oil and lime juice. This can be done in advance.

Take advice as to whether your ham needs soaking or not. It will if particularly salty – your butcher or the meat counter at your supermarket should be able to tell you. I tend to forget about an overnight soak and instead cover the ham in cold water, bring to the boil, then immediately pour off the liquid, re-cover the ham and start again.

When you are ready to start cooking proper, put the ham in a pot – you want it to be quite a snug fit – and pour over the Ting or Lilt and the beer. Bring to the boil, skim the ham until any foam turns white, then add all the rest of the aromatics.

continued…

Main courses

98

continued…

Partially cover, then leave to simmer, fairly gently, for approximately 1½ hours. By this point the ham should be tender. Strain the ham, reserving the cooking liquor, and leave to rest for 15 minutes, lightly covered with foil.

Heat a large griddle pan and a frying pan. Whisk the rum with the honey and brush over the pineapple and grapefruit slices. When the griddle is too hot to hold your hand over, grill the fruit for a couple of minutes on each side until nicely caramelized with char lines.

Cut the ham into thick slices. Put in the frying pan in a single layer and ladle over some of the stock. Simmer for a couple of minutes just to warm through and soften.

Serve with the pineapple, grapefruit and sweetcorn fritters (see below, or salsa).

Makes about 8

3 eggs

1 tbsp light soy sauce

300g/generous 2 cups sweetcorn (corn kernels)

4 spring onions (scallions), very finely chopped

1 red chilli, finely chopped

2 tbsp finely chopped coriander (cilantro)

Finely grated zest of 1 lime

75g/½ cup plus 1 tbsp plain (all-purpose) flour

Oil, for frying

Sea salt and freshly ground black pepper

Sweetcorn fritters

In a bowl, beat the eggs with the soy sauce, then mix in the sweetcorn (corn kernels), spring onions (scallions), chilli, coriander (cilantro) and lime zest. Season with salt and pepper. Sift in the flour and mix into a smooth batter. Heat a frying pan and cover the base with oil, then add dollops of the sweetcorn batter, well spaced out – you should manage to cook 5 at a time. Flatten down slightly, fry for a couple of minutes until well browned, then flip and cook for a further minute.

Sautéed Chicken Thighs with Lemon, Mustard and Basil

Serves 4

1 tbsp olive oil

15g/1 tbsp butter

8 chicken thighs, bone in and skin on

1 onion, finely chopped

2 garlic cloves, finely chopped

100ml/7 tbsp white wine

Finely grated zest of 1 lemon and
   juice of 2 lemons

1 tbsp Dijon mustard

100ml/7 tbsp water

1 tbsp capers, rinsed

A large handful of basil, roughly torn

Sea salt and freshly ground black
   pepper

This is one of my favourite supper dishes – it's relatively quick, uses mainly storecupboard ingredients, and doesn't need much accompaniment. I might serve it with mashed potatoes or steamed new potatoes, with a floppy green lettuce or green beans.

Heat the olive oil and butter in a large, shallow flameproof casserole or pan. When the butter is foaming, add the chicken thighs, skin side down, and fry until they are well browned – do not stint on this, it will take at least 10 minutes. Remove the chicken from the pan, then add the onion and sauté on a gentle heat until soft and translucent. Add the garlic and cook for a further minute or two.

Turn up the heat and add the wine. Bring to the boil and allow the wine to bubble off, then stir in the lemon zest and juice and the mustard. Add the water, return the chicken to the pan, skin side up, and season with salt and pepper. Cook, partially covered, until the thighs are cooked through. Add a splash more water if necessary.

Remove the chicken from the pan again then stir in the capers and basil. Spoon the sauce over the chicken and serve immediately.

Poached Chicken with Lemon and Sorrel Sauce

Serves 4

1 chicken

A few pared pieces of lemon zest

A few peppercorns

1 onion, quartered

1 carrot, roughly chopped

½ head garlic

Sea salt and ground white pepper

For the sauce

15g/1 tbsp butter

A small bunch of sorrel, leaves only, shredded

300ml/1¼ cups whipping (heavy) cream

A squeeze of lemon juice

Creamy sauces such as this one are normally served with poached chicken breasts, but I'm afraid I am not a fan of these – it is just so much better to poach a whole chicken. It gives you cooking liquor, chicken for leftovers and a pick of white or brown meat, both of which will be happy with a dousing of this sauce. Sorrel is included here for its very citrusy notes, but I can't resist adding a squeeze of lemon juice too.

First poach the chicken. If you don't want a very fatty broth, remove some of the chicken skin – at least that which covers the breasts and thighs. Pull out some of the fat you will find around the cavity opening too. Put into a pot – it should be a snug fit – then add the aromatics and vegetables. Pour in enough water (or chicken stock) so that the thickest part of the legs are covered. Season with salt, then bring to the boil. Skim until any foam slowly turns from mushroom grey to white. Reduce the heat to the slowest possible simmer, then cover. Simmer for 45 minutes, then remove from the heat and leave to stand for a further 15 minutes. Leave until you are ready to serve, reserving 50ml/3½ tbsp of the cooking liquor for the sauce.

For the sauce, melt the butter and add the sorrel. When it has completely collapsed into a purée, remove from the heat. In a separate pan, heat the cream and reserved chicken cooking liquor until just at boiling point. Add the cooked sorrel, then season well with salt and white pepper. Add a squeeze of lemon juice. Serve with slices of the poached chicken.

Bergamot and Lemon Roast Chicken

Serves 4

1 chicken

Pared zest and juice of 1 bergamot

A few sprigs of tarragon

A few sprigs of thyme

½ head garlic, cloves separated and
left unpeeled

50g/3½ tbsp butter, softened

125ml/generous ½ cup vermouth

125ml/generous ½ cup water

300ml/1¼ cups chicken stock

½ tsp runny honey (optional)

Sea salt

A classic lemony roast chicken is hard to beat, but any particularly fragrant, acidic citrus will also help chicken shine. The bergamot is subtle, but this is exactly what you need – it enhances the chicken flavour, adds an elusive perfume, and will help add depth to any resulting stock and soup. One to cook in the middle of winter when you need a bit of uplift in your life.

Sprinkle the inside and out of the chicken with salt and, if you have time, leave to air dry, uncovered, in the refrigerator overnight. This is not essential, but does improve texture. Either way, remove from the refrigerator an hour before you want to cook it so it can start cooking from room temperature. Preheat the oven to 230°C/450°F/Gas mark 8.

Put most of the pared bergamot zest in the cavity of the chicken, with half of each herb. Put the remaining zest, herbs and garlic in the bottom of a roasting tin and place the chicken on top. Rub the skin all over with the butter, then sprinkle with half the bergamot juice. Pour in the vermouth and water.

Roast for 15 minutes, then turn down to 200°C/400°F/Gas mark 6 and roast for a further 45 minutes. Check the chicken is done – if not, roast for a further 5–10 minutes. Remove from the roasting tin to a platter and leave to rest.

For the gravy, remove the herbs, zest and garlic from the tin and spoon off any fat. Squish the flesh out of all the garlic cloves and add to the roasting tin juices. Put the tin over a low heat and stir until you have scraped up any brown bits on the base. Add the stock and most of the rest of the bergamot juice. Taste before adding the honey, if you think the sauce could do with extra sweetness. Bring to the boil. When the chicken has rested for 20 minutes, add any juices which have been released during that time. Return the sauce to the boil and add the remaining bergamot juice to freshen it up.

Mandarin Chicken with Giant Couscous and Charred Broccoli

Serves 4

2 onions, peeled and cut into thin wedges

2 tbsp olive oil

8–10 chicken thighs, bone in and skin on

Finely grated zest and juice of 3 mandarins

Finely grated zest and juice of 1 lime or ½ lemon

2 garlic cloves, finely chopped

A few sprigs of thyme or rosemary

100ml/7 tbsp vermouth

Sea salt and freshly ground black pepper

For the couscous

1 head of broccoli, cut into small florets, rinsed and drained

2 tbsp olive oil

Finely grated zest of 1 lemon

1 red chilli, finely chopped

200g/1⅓ cups giant couscous

500ml/2 cups plus 1 tbsp water or chicken stock

50g/⅔ cup flaked (slivered) or nibbed almonds, lightly toasted

Variation

You don't have to make this with giant couscous – a quick couscous, rice or some potatoes would be just as good.

A family favourite, and easy enough for a simple midweek supper. If you can start marinating the chicken first thing in the morning, ready to cook at night, that is ideal; otherwise just a few minutes while the onions are cooking will be enough to help the flavours along.

Preheat the oven to 200°C/400°F/Gas mark 6. Put the onions in the base of a roasting tin and drizzle over a tablespoon of the olive oil. Add a splash of water to the tin and roast in the oven for 10 minutes.

Put the chicken thighs in a bowl and season well with salt and pepper. Rub in the mandarin and lime or lemon zests.

Remove the tin from the oven and give the onions a good stir – they should be well on their way to softening with very little colour. Sprinkle over the garlic, making sure most of it falls in the centre of the tin, then add the thyme or rosemary.

Arrange the chicken thighs over the onions. Whisk the vermouth with the citrus juices then pour this around the chicken. Drizzle over the remaining olive oil. Roast in the oven for 45 minutes, until the chicken is cooked through with a crisp golden skin and the liquid is syrupy.

Meanwhile, make the couscous. Toss the broccoli florets with a tablespoon of the oil. Arrange on a baking tray and sprinkle with salt, the lemon zest and chilli. Put in the oven, below the chicken, preferably with some space in between the two, and roast for 20 minutes. Remove from the oven – it should be lightly charred.

To cook the couscous, heat the remaining olive oil in a saucepan. Add the couscous and toast for a few minutes. Pour in the water or stock and cook gently, stirring, until all the liquid is absorbed and the couscous is soft, about 15 minutes. Check regularly and add a little more liquid if necessary towards the end if the couscous isn't yet done.

Toss the couscous with the broccoli and the almonds. Serve with the chicken, with the citrusy sauce and onions spooned over.

Marinated Chicken with Charred Limes, Saffron Butter and Soft Flatbreads

Serves 4

1 chicken (or 2 poussin), each cut
  into 10 pieces, skin on

A large pinch of saffron strands

1 tbsp boiling water

100g/scant ½ cup butter

1 garlic clove, crushed

Sea salt and freshly ground black
  pepper

For the marinade

A large pinch of saffron strands

1 tbsp boiling water

250ml/generous 1 cup lime juice
  (or sour orange or lemon)

1 onion, coarsely grated

For the cucumber and yogurt sauce

200ml/generous ¾ cup yogurt

A handful of mint leaves, finely
  chopped

½ cucumber, peeled, halved lengthways,
  deseeded, grated and drained

A pinch of sugar

To serve

4 limes, halved

Soft Flatbreads (see page 108)

Flat-leaf parsley, chopped

Lime-Pickled Red Onions (see page 26)

Sally Butcher and her husband Jamshid kindly talked me through this recipe, which is a Middle Eastern classic. Poussin are skinned, cut up and left to sit in a bath of lime juice for 24 hours, before they are grilled or barbecued, basted all the while with saffron butter. Persians normally use a concentrated bottled juice for this which is seriously sherbety and a bit of an acquired taste. Use this or a regular bottled sort – or if you can find a use for zest (there are plenty of ideas dotted around this book!) use around 12–15 large limes.

Put the chicken in a refrigerator-friendly receptacle. Season generously with salt and pepper. Using a pestle and mortar, grind the saffron for the marinade with a pinch of salt and mix with the boiling water. Add to the citrus juice and pour the lot over the chicken or poussins, along with the onion. Refrigerate and marinate overnight.

The next day, either get your barbecue ready or heat your oven to its highest temperature. Grind and soak the saffron in the boiling water, as before, and put it in a saucepan with the butter and garlic. Melt together.

Drain and pat dry the chicken pieces then either arrange over your barbecue or a baking tray. Baste with the butter and cook for 10 minutes. Baste again, cook for a further 10 minutes, then repeat. By this time the chicken should be cooked through and nicely browned and blistered. Reheat any remaining butter.

Put the limes on the barbecue or on a griddle pan for a couple of minutes.

Mix the yogurt with the mint and grated cucumber, and season with salt and a pinch of sugar.

To serve, warm through the flatbreads. Serve the chicken torn from the bone and piled into flatbreads with the yogurt, any leftover basting butter, parsley, pickled onions and squeezes of the charred limes.

Soft Flatbreads

Makes 8

500g/3½–3⅔ cups strong white flour
(plain/all-purpose flour also works)

10g/⅓oz instant dried yeast

1 tsp sugar

1 tsp salt

150g/⅔ cup yogurt

200ml/¾ cup plus 1 tbsp hot water
from the kettle

15g/1 tbsp olive oil or melted butter

Melted butter, for brushing

Sesame or poppy seeds, for sprinkling
(optional)

These are round, pocketless pittas that are ideal for folding in half and filling (as you would tacos). The trick is to get the temperature right as they need to be cooked through, but remain soft and pliable so they will fold easily. This is the same basic recipe I use for naan breads too, so you can pull them into a slightly thinner teardrop shape, and cook on a hotter heat.

Put the flour in a bowl and mix in the yeast and sugar. Sprinkle over the salt. Whisk the yogurt and hot water together – you should end up with a liquid that is tepid. Add this to the flour along with the olive oil or butter. Mix thoroughly to a soft, very slightly sticky dough. Turn out onto an oiled surface and knead until the dough is smooth. Return to the bowl and cover with a damp tea towel or plastic wrap and leave to double in size.

Turn out the dough again and divide into 8 even pieces. Roll into rounds of approximately 20cm/8-in diameter.

Heat a griddle, skillet or frying pan until it is fairly hot – you don't want it as hot as it will go or the flatbread will just blister and blacken on the outside before it's cooked within, and will consequently be too hard to fold. Add a dough round and cook for 2–3 minutes on each side – it should be cooked through, lightly browned/charred and still pliable. Brush with melted butter and sprinkle with seeds, if you like. Keep warm in a basket lined with a tea towel or cloth and cover while you cook the rest.

Mojo Chicken

Serves 4

4 boneless, skinless chicken
  breasts, butterflied

2 green or semi-ripe plantain

Juice of 1 lime

15g/1 tbsp butter

A few coriander (cilantro) leaves

For the marinade

1 onion, finely chopped

1 head of garlic, cloves peeled and
  finely chopped

1 Scotch bonnet or other hot chilli,
  deseeded and finely chopped

A small bunch of coriander (cilantro)

1 tsp dried oregano

1 tsp fresh thyme leaves

1 tsp ground cumin

A pinch of ground allspice

300ml/1¼ cups sour orange juice

Finely grated zest and juice of 1 lime

100ml/7 tbsp water

50ml/3½ tbsp olive oil

Sea salt

I love recipes in which the marinade can also be used as
a sauce, as it is much less wasteful. This is loosely based
on a Cuban mojo sauce and really should be made
with sour oranges. If that is impossible, use one third
sweet oranges, one third lemon juice, one third lime. To
temper the hot, sour, salty notes of the sauce, serve with
something slightly sweet such as the Lime and Coconut
Rice on page 145. Fried plantain also helps with this.

Put all the marinade ingredients with plenty of salt into
a food processor or blender and pulse until relatively
smooth. Place the chicken breasts in a shallow dish, pour
over the marinade, cover then leave in the refrigerator for
several hours or overnight.

When you are ready to cook the chicken, scrape off as
much of the marinade as you can into a small saucepan.
Heat your barbecue and grill the chicken for 3–4 minutes
on each side until just cooked through. (Alternatively, use
a griddle pan, making sure it is extremely hot when you
start cooking; I heat mine for at least 10 minutes on a
high heat.)

Meanwhile, bring the marinade to the boil and simmer for
10 minutes, adding a splash of water if it looks as though
it is in danger of reducing down too far – you don't want
it too syrupy.

Peel the plantain (or in practice cut through and break
off the skin) and cut into slices on the diagonal,
dropping them into the lime juice as you slice them.
Heat the butter in a frying pan until melted, then add
the plantain slices. Cook until each side is golden brown.
Drain on kitchen paper.

Serve the chicken with the marinade, the plantain and a
few coriander (cilantro) leaves as garnish.

Seville Orange-Spiced Duck

Serves 4

2 duck breasts, cut in half

4 duck legs, separated into thigh
and drumstick

1 head of garlic, cloves peeled and
finely chopped

50g/1¾oz fresh root ginger, peeled
and finely chopped

500ml/generous 2 cups freshly
squeezed orange juice

2 tbsp fish sauce

2 tsp palm sugar or soft light
brown sugar

2 star anise

3 bird's-eye red chillies

3 lemongrass stalks, peeled, whites
finely chopped

A bunch of spring onions (scallions)
white parts only (save the green parts
for serving), shredded lengthways

Sea salt and freshly ground black
pepper

To serve

Reserved green parts of spring
onions, shredded

1 tsp sesame seeds

A few drops of sesame oil

Coriander (cilantro), to garnish

This is the second recipe I have purloined from my pressure cooker book. I look to the intro and see that the recipe even converted my husband who "does not normally like orange in savoury dishes". How times have changed – these days oranges feature prominently and he never takes issue. Perhaps this is an example of the theory that if you try something at least 10–12 times you will come to like it?

Heat a large, heavy-based frying pan and fry the duck pieces, skin side down, until they are crisp, brown, and much of the fat has rendered out. You will probably have to do this in a couple of batches.

Spoon off a tablespoon of the duck fat and add it to a large flameproof casserole – the rest of the duck fat can be chilled for future use. Add the garlic and ginger and fry until they smell aromatic and are only just starting to take on some colour. Add the rest of the ingredients, with salt and lots of pepper. Place the duck pieces, skin side up, in the cooking liquor and bring to the boil. Turn down the heat, then partially cover. Leave to cook for around 1½ hours, until the duck is tender.

Remove the duck from the casserole and keep warm. Try to spoon off any excess fat – if it proves tricky, you can always strain the liquid first, reserve the solids, and add them back when you have taken off the fat. Bring the liquor back to the boil and reduce until syrupy. Add the duck pieces back to the sauce, making sure they are warmed through.

Sprinkle with the spring onion (scallion) greens, sesame seeds, a dash of sesame oil and coriander (cilantro). Best served with some jasmine rice and steamed or stir-fried greens.

Classic Duck à l'Orange

Serves 4

1 duck, around 1.6–1.8kg/3½–4lb

1 tbsp brandy or eau de vie

1 Seville orange, quartered

A few sprigs of thyme

4 bay leaves

1 onion, peeled and sliced into
   thick wedges

Sea salt and finely ground
   white pepper

For the sauce

3 Seville oranges

50g/¼ cup granulated sugar

50ml/3½ tbsp water

1 tbsp white wine vinegar

2 shallots, finely chopped

200ml/generous ¾ cup well reduced
   chicken stock (or duck if you have it)

This got a bit of a bad rep at one stage, thanks to neon gloopy sauces and lurid 1970s presentation. In fact, I wasn't sure about whether I wanted to cook it, especially as so many of the recipes are very involved. Even Jane Grigson, whom I usually view as a beacon of good sense and pragmatism, has a system of complicated rigs and a time-consuming use of a hairdryer to help get the crispest of crisp duck skins.

I succumbed in the end and found that the duck and sour orange combination is one that should be celebrated. If you want to make this out of season (although it seems to me to be a very wintry sort of dish), you can take a shortcut with the sauce and just enrich with Seville orange marmalade. Alternatively, try using grapefruit – or perhaps even Ugli Duckling?

Preheat the oven to 200°C/400°F/Gas mark 6. Prick all over the skin of the duck with a skewer or fork, making sure you focus on the fattiest parts and trying not to pierce the flesh. Put the duck on a rack in your sink and pour over 2 kettles of boiling water. Pat the duck dry, then rub over the brandy. Sprinkle with salt and finely ground white pepper.

Put the Seville orange quarters inside the cavity of the duck along with half the thyme and one of the bay leaves. Put the remaining thyme in the bottom of a roasting tin and top with the onion and remaining bay leaves. Place the duck on top, breast side down, then roast for 30 minutes. Turn the duck breast side up and roast for a further 50 minutes. Remove from the oven and leave to rest. If you want to serve it jointed, this is the time to do so, otherwise you can leave it whole and carve at the table.

continued...

continued...

To make the sauce, use a swivel peeler to pare the zest from one of the Seville oranges in strips as long as you can manage. Cut into a julienne, then blanch in boiling water for 3 minutes. Juice all the oranges and set aside.

Put the sugar and water in a saucepan and heat gently until the sugar has dissolved. Add the blanched orange zest and continue to cook gently for another 3–4 minutes until the mixture is syrupy. Remove the zest from the syrup, reserving it, and add the vinegar. Turn up the heat and boil until the sugar caramelizes and turns the colour of amber. Add the shallots and the orange juice. The caramel will probably seize up and spit at you, so be careful. Stir until it has dissolved again, then add the stock. Simmer until the sauce is well reduced but not too thick. Taste and adjust for seasoning – you can add a little more orange juice or stock at this point if you think it needs it.

When the duck has rested, strain off any liquid from the pan and remove the fat, then add these juices to the sauce. Simmer until piping hot and add the zest back to the sauce.

Duck Soup with Noodles

Even after feeding four people, I often find enough meat left on a duck to be eked out with a soup. This is one of my favourite soups to make with the carcass.

Take off every scrap of meat you can find on the duck and put to one side. Make a stock with the carcass, adding a couple of star anise, an onion, carrot and a couple of sticks of celery, a few peppercorns and bay leaves. Include any leftover scrapings from the roasting tin as well as some pared sour orange zest. Cover with water, bring to the boil and skim, then either pressure cook for 25 minutes or simmer gently for around 1½ hours. Strain and leave to chill so you can remove any fat.

To make the soup, put the stock in a saucepan. Add 2 sliced garlic cloves, a 2cm/¾-in piece of fresh root ginger, finely chopped, and 1 red chilli. Slice a bunch of spring onions (scallions) on the diagonal. Add the whites and reserve the greens for a garnish. Add 100g/3½oz mushrooms and 4 heads of oriental greens. Simmer and taste for seasoning. Add soy sauce and a little mirin or sake. Cook 200g/7oz noodles according to the packet instructions and refresh under cold water to stop them cooking. Dress with a little sesame oil. Add the duck and noodles to the soup along with lots of fresh coriander (cilantro). Serve with any type of "kosho" if you have any, or make a ponzu sauce as on page 92, with the spring onion greens sprinkled on top.

Sautéed Chicken Livers with Marsala and Orange

Serves 2

1 tsp olive oil

15g/1 tbsp butter

1 large onion, sliced

1 garlic clove, finely chopped

1 red chilli, finely chopped

400g/14oz chicken livers, trimmed

50ml/3½ tbsp sweet Marsala

1 large orange, segmented (see page 15), peel and membranes reserved

Sea salt and freshly ground black pepper

To serve

Sourdough toast, buttered

A handful of parsley, finely chopped (optional)

Chicken livers are a regular fast lunch for my husband and me on the days we both work from home, and I throw in whatever I have to hand. On this particular day I used Marsala in place of the more usual vermouth – and my husband said it was the best plate of liver he'd ever eaten so we've stuck with it.

Heat the olive oil and butter in a large frying pan until the butter has melted. Add the onion, garlic and chilli and sauté on a medium heat for several minutes until softening and turning a very light golden brown. Push the onion and garlic to one side and add the liver. Cook for 2–3 minutes on each side. Season with salt and pepper.

Turn up the heat and add the Marsala. Allow to boil down for around 30 seconds, then add the orange segments. Take the reserved orange peel and membranes and squeeze any excess juice over the livers. Serve with some buttered sourdough toast and a sprinkling of parsley, if you like.

Black-Eyed Peas with Lime and Chipotle

Serves 4

1 tbsp coconut oil

2 red onions, sliced

2 celery sticks, sliced

1 red (bell) pepper, cut into strips

1 green (bell) pepper, cut into strips

2 garlic cloves, finely chopped

1 tsp ground cumin

1 tsp ground coriander

½ tsp chipotle powder

1 tsp dried oregano

500g/1⅓ cups cooked black-eyed beans (peas)

1 x 400ml tin/1¾ cups coconut milk

Finely grated zest and juice of 1 lime

200g/7oz sprouting broccoli or coarsely shredded spring greens

Sea salt and freshly ground black pepper

For the eggs

1 tbsp olive or coconut oil

4 eggs

Juice of 1 lime

A sprinkling of chipotle powder

To serve

Coriander (cilantro) leaves

Warm corn tortillas (optional; nice but not at all necessary)

This is a favourite brunch dish in our house – the lime and chilli enliven what is otherwise a quite sweetly unchallenging dish. A savoury combination of eggs and citrus works surprisingly well. The Greeks fry eggs in olive oil then douse liberally in lemon juice, a combination that is addictive once tried. This is similar in concept, using lime juice and chilli instead.

Heat the coconut oil in a large, lidded frying pan. Add the onions, celery and both (bell) peppers, then cook for several minutes on a medium heat until starting to brown around the edges.

Add the garlic, spices and oregano, then stir for a couple more minutes before adding the beans (peas), coconut milk and lime zest. Season with salt and pepper and cook for 5 minutes, uncovered, on a low heat. Add the sprouting broccoli or spring greens, then cover again and cook for a further 6–7 minutes until the greens are tender.

Add half the lime juice and taste, then add more if you think it is necessary.

Heat the olive or coconut oil in a frying pan, add the eggs and fry until they are cooked as you like, then drench in lime juice and sprinkle over some chipotle. Serve the beans and greens with the fried eggs and warm tortillas, if you like, generously garnished with coriander (cilantro) leaves.

Grilled Aubergines with Mozzarella and Yuzukosho

Serves 4

3 fat, round aubergines (eggplants), cut into 2cm/¾-in rounds

Olive oil, for brushing

250g/9oz mozzarella, thickly sliced and drained in a colander

A little yuzu powder, for sprinkling (optional)

Sea salt and freshly ground black pepper

For the dressing

1 tbsp yuzukosho, or other type of kosho

1 tbsp yuzu juice or lemon juice

Finely grated zest and juice of 1 mandarin (optional)

A dash of light soy sauce

For the greens and lentils

1 tbsp oil

2 spring onions (scallions), sliced diagonally

1 garlic clove, finely chopped

200g/7oz chard, stems and leaves separated, both sliced

100g/3½oz sprouting broccoli, cut into sections

100g/3½oz oriental greens, sliced lengthways

50g/1¾oz mizuna or any other mustardy greens

A handful of shiso leaves (optional)

100g/⅔ cup cooked green lentils (preferably al dente)

A dash of light soy sauce or tamari (optional)

I'm venturing into the murky realms of fusion here. This is a combination I tried on a fridge forage and I loved it – the aubergines (eggplants) are smoky and squidgy, the mozzarella is creamy and the dressing has just the right amount of hot, sweet, saltiness to offset any richness. Also, if you use, for example, the lemon-mandarin combination for kosho as described on page 24, you are still – just – in the world of Mediterranean flavours. Don't use the best mozzarella here as it will ooze; a cheap one actually works better.

First, grill or bake the aubergine (eggplant) slices. If you have the time to grill them on a griddle, do so, as you get the best smoky flavour that way, otherwise you can put them under a medium grill or even bake in the oven at 200°C/400°F/Gas mark 6 for 20 minutes. Whichever way you do it, brush first with olive oil and sprinkle with salt. Cook until they are browned, with char lines if on a griddle, and beautifully tender within.

While the aubergines are grilling, whisk the dressing ingredients together and taste. Adjust by adding more of any of the ingredients until you get the flavour you like.

To finish the aubergines, put them all on a baking tray and lay the mozzarella on top. Put under a hot grill for as short a time as possible, so the mozzarella browns lightly but is still soft and not too rubbery.

Meanwhile, for the greens, put the oil in a wok and heat until shimmering. Add the spring onions (scallions), garlic, chard stems and sprouting broccoli and stir fry for 2–3 minutes, until the broccoli is almost cooked. Add the chard leaves and oriental greens with a splash of water (or stock) and cook for a further minute. Add the mizuna and shiso leaves, if using, and wilt in, then stir through the lentils just to warm them. Season with salt and pepper, and a dash of soy sauce or tamari if you like.

Sprinkle the mozzarella-topped aubergines with yuzu powder if you have some, and serve with the dressing, alongside the greens and lentils in a separate bowl.

Early Summer Vegetables with Lime and Tarragon

Serves 4

For the vegetables

15g/1 tbsp butter

200g/7oz baby new potatoes, halved

2 small leeks, sliced

50ml/3½ tbsp white wine or vermouth

300g/10½oz fresh baby broad beans (fava beans), podded

A bunch or 2 of asparagus, cut on the diagonal into lengths

2–3 courgettes (zucchini) or patty pans, sliced into rounds or wedges

500g/1lb 2oz fresh peas, podded (reserve the pods)

Sea salt and black pepper

For the stock

Reserved pea pods

Trimmings from the asparagus

Trimmings from the leeks

1 large sprig of tarragon

2 pieces of pared lime zest

2 lemon verbena or lemon balm leaves (optional)

½ tsp fennel seeds

½ tsp peppercorns

For the lime and tarragon oil

50ml/3½ tbsp olive oil

Finely grated zest and juice of 1 lime

Leaves from a large sprig of tarragon

To serve

Fresh ricotta or other creamy cheese

A few mint, basil or verbena leaves

If you happen to have a lemon or lime tree (not a kaffir, these are too strong here), adding the leaves to the stock instead of the lime zest will give a beautifully subtle flavour which really works well with young vegetables. Depending on the time of year, I will garnish this with feathery fennel and borage flowers from the garden.

First make a quick stock. Put the pea pods, asparagus and leek trimmings left over from preparing the vegetables into a medium saucepan, along with the tarragon, lime zest or leaves and verbena or lemon balm leaves, if using. Add the spices, then cover with cold water – only about 600ml/2½ cups. Bring to the boil, then turn down the heat and leave to simmer for 15 minutes. Strain through a double layer of muslin.

Melt the butter in a saucepan or flameproof casserole over a medium heat, then add the potatoes and leeks. Season with plenty of salt, then pour in the wine or vermouth. Allow this to almost completely boil off, then turn down the heat, cover, and leave to braise gently for around 10 minutes. Add 500ml/just over 2 cups of the stock and cook for a further 5 minutes. Add the broad beans (fava beans), asparagus and courgettes (zucchini) and simmer for a few minutes until just al dente, then add the peas – if they are very fresh and young, they will barely need cooking.

To make the oil, put in a food processor with the lime zest and juice, and the tarragon. Season with salt and pepper and blitz until the oil is green flecked. Serve the vegetables with a tiny amount of the broth to keep them moist, with large spoonfuls of ricotta, a sprinkling of herbs and the oil drizzled over.

Orange-Roasted Root Vegetables with Herb and Lemon Pesto

Serves 4

4 large carrots, peeled and cut into thick batons

2–3 large parsnips, peeled and cut into thick batons

1 small celeriac, peeled and cut into wedges

2 onions, peeled and cut into wedges

A few sprigs of thyme

Finely grated zest of ½ orange and juice of 2 oranges

1 tbsp red wine vinegar

2 tbsp olive oil

1 tsp runny honey (optional)

Sea salt and freshly ground black pepper

For the pesto

50g/about ⅓ cup pistachios or almonds

1 tsp coriander seeds

A small bunch of dill

A small bunch of mint, leaves only

A small to medium bunch of parsley

1 garlic clove, peeled

Finely grated zest and juice of 1 lemon

50ml/3½ tbsp olive oil

For the couscous

150g/generous ¾ cup couscous

150ml/10 tbsp tepid water

Juice of 1 orange

A drizzle of olive oil

This is a particularly adaptable recipe as you can add any type of root vegetable you like. I happen to love the combination of orange and honeyed carrots and parsnips.

The pesto is versatile – you can stir it into pasta, drop it into soup or serve with any grilled meat or fish. As written, it is vegan and I think it is better that way – the addition of hard cheese can muddy the flavours.

Preheat the oven to 200°C/400°F/Gas mark 6.

Put all the vegetables in a large roasting tin. Tuck in the sprigs of thyme, pour over the orange juice and red wine vinegar. Toss to coat the vegetables, then repeat with the olive oil, orange zest and plenty of salt.

Roast for 30 minutes, loosely covered with foil, then remove the foil and roast for a further 30 minutes, turning the vegetables over every so often. Drizzle over the honey, if using, then continue to roast for 15–20 minutes until the vegetables are tender and nicely browned or charred around the edges.

To make the pesto, put the pistachios or almonds and the coriander seeds in a food processor and blitz briefly to coarsely grind. Add all the remaining ingredients and season generously with salt and pepper. Blitz until you have a fairly coarse sauce, a little thinner than regular pesto – if it is very thick still, add more lemon juice or a splash of water.

Make the couscous by putting it in a bowl and pouring over the water and orange juice. Add salt and a drizzle of olive oil. Leave to stand until all the liquid has absorbed and the couscous is tender, then fork through to fluff up.

Serve the roast vegetables with the couscous, and the pesto drizzled over both.

Linguine with Lemon and Asparagus

Serves 4

250g/9oz linguine (or spaghetti
  at a pinch)

300g/10½oz asparagus, trimmed

Olive oil, for drizzling

30g/2 tbsp butter

Finely grated zest and juice of
  1 large lemon

4 egg yolks

50g/1¾oz hard cheese, such as
  Parmesan or Pecorino

Sea salt and freshly ground black
  pepper

A very simple dish, reliant on good ingredients, so wait until early summer when asparagus is abundant and you can get large, sweet, fragrant lemons from Italy. I specify a "hard cheese" here – I would normally use Parmesan or Pecorino in this recipe, but if you are vegetarian it is now easy to find rennet-free alternatives.

Bring a large pot of water to the boil and salt generously. Add the linguine and cook until just al dente. Drain, reserving a small cupful of the cooking liquid.

Meanwhile, heat a griddle pan until it is as hot as you can get it – it should be too hot to hold your hand over comfortably. Wash the asparagus, shake off the excess liquid and put on the griddle. Drizzle with a little olive oil and grill for 3–4 minutes on each side. Remove and slice each spear in half on the diagonal.

Melt the butter in the pasta pan then add the lemon zest. Turn the heat down as low as you can, then whisk the lemon juice and egg yolks into the butter, until you have an emulsion. Add some of the reserved pasta liquid, a tablespoon at a time, until you have a sauce the texture of single (light) cream – it should be silky-smooth and just coat the pasta when you add it without being cloying. Add the pasta and asparagus to the pan and toss to coat in the sauce.

Serve with plenty of black pepper and the cheese shaved over the top.

Citrus Risotto

Serves 4

1–1.2 litres/4–5 cups vegetable stock

1 tbsp olive oil

50g/3½ tbsp butter

1 small onion, very finely chopped

2 garlic cloves, finely chopped

Finely grated zest and juice of 1 lemon

A few sprigs of tarragon, finely chopped
  (optional)

300g/1½ cups Arborio rice

100ml/7 tbsp white wine

Sea salt and freshly ground black
  pepper

To garnish

1 tbsp olive oil

2 red chillies, finely chopped or sliced

2 tbsp capers

A handful of basil leaves, shredded

This is a vegetarian recipe, but don't feel limited
– whilst I love it on its own, I will also make it to
complement grilled shrimp or scallops. A risotto should
have a comforting mellow creaminess about it, which
this certainly does – but if you want to pep it up, do
add the optional fried chilli and capers to drizzle over
at the end.

Lemon is the most common citrus to add to risotto,
there to enhance flavour rather than to dominate.
However, please try adding mandarin as well, or swap
the lemon for grapefruit, and pair with thyme or
rosemary in place of the tarragon – the results
are superb.

Place the stock in a large saucepan and warm through
until just below boiling point. Keep at this temperature.

Heat the oil and half the butter in a large, straight sided
frying pan. Add the onion and sauté gently until very soft
and translucent. Add the garlic, lemon zest and tarragon,
if using, and continue to cook for a minute, then stir in
the rice. When the rice is completely coated in the butter
and oil – it will look glossy – add the wine. Turn up the
heat and let the wine boil off then season with salt, and
a little pepper if you like. Add half the lemon juice, then
start adding the warm stock a ladleful at a time, stirring
between each addition until it is incorporated. When most
of the stock is incorporated you should find that when you
pull your spoon through the rice you will see a clean pan
base before the rice slowly flows back around it. At this
point, it should be just al dente and creamy. Beat in the
remaining butter, then taste and add more lemon juice if
you feel the risotto needs it.

For the garnish, heat the olive oil in a small frying pan.
When it is very hot, add the chillies and capers and flash
fry for just a few seconds. Serve this, and lots of shredded
basil, with the risotto.

Braised New Potatoes and Porcini Mushrooms with Lemon and Rosemary

Serves 4

30g/1oz dried porcini mushrooms (or similar)

100ml/7 tbsp warm water

1 lemon, very thinly sliced into rounds, each round cut into quarters

50ml/3½ tbsp olive oil

3 shallots, sliced

750g/1lb 10oz new or waxy potatoes, scrubbed and sliced into 3mm/ ⅛-in rounds

300g/10½oz fresh mushrooms, preferably field, thickly sliced

2 garlic cloves, sliced

A few sprigs of rosemary

100ml/7 tbsp white wine, vermouth or Marsala

Sea salt and freshly ground black pepper

The one season that does not have an overabundance of citrus recipes is autumn. This one is an exception – the lemon flavour is pronounced and really lifts the earthy flavour of the mushrooms. If using sliced lemons feels like too much, you can use the zest and juice of a lemon instead, adding it in with the mushroom liquor. Other earthy root vegetables, such as celeriac or Jerusalem artichokes, can be used in place of, or in addition to, the potatoes.

Cover the dried mushrooms with the warm water and leave to soak until plumped up and softened. Strain, reserving any non-gritty soaking liquor, then roughly chop.

Put the lemon pieces in a saucepan and cover with cold water. Bring to the boil and simmer for 5 minutes. Drain.

Heat half the olive oil in a heavy-based flameproof casserole. Add the shallots and fry on a medium heat until softened and lightly browned. Add the potatoes and continue to cook for another 5 minutes, then add the fresh and the rehydrated mushrooms. Continue to cook for a few more minutes, then stir in the garlic, rosemary and lemon slices.

Pour in the wine, vermouth or Marsala and allow to bubble down to almost nothing, then add the reserved mushroom liquor. Season with salt and pepper, then bring to the boil before turning down to the gentlest of simmers. Cover and cook until the potatoes are just tender – they and the mushrooms will braise, creating their own liquid.

When the potatoes are tender, drizzle with more of the oil, then put under a preheated grill until the top layer of potatoes is golden brown. Serve with greens.

Roast Vegetables with Feta and Orange

Serves 4

3 small red onions, peeled and quartered

2 red (bell) peppers, cut into strips

1 green (bell) pepper, cut into strips

2 courgettes (zucchini), cut into chunks on the diagonal

200g/7oz piece of pumpkin, cut into thin wedges

1 head of garlic, cloves separated, unpeeled

A handful of oregano leaves, plus extra to serve

2 whole oranges plus the juice of 2 medium oranges

2 tbsp olive oil

75g/¾ cup black olives

400g/14oz feta, broken into chunks

Sea salt and freshly ground black pepper

Parsley leaves, to serve

I think this is substantial enough on its own, but you could add a side salad if you like, or some leftover grains of some sort.

I don't eat the skin of the oranges unless it is particularly thin, but somehow the orange does taste better roasted when left unpeeled.

Preheat the oven to 200°C/400°F/Gas mark 6.

Put all the vegetables into a large roasting tin and sprinkle in the garlic cloves and oregano. Top and tail the 2 whole oranges then cut into fairly thick slices. Cut each slice into quarters. Add all this orange to the roasting tin, then pour over the orange juice. Season with salt and pepper and drizzle everything with the olive oil.

Roast in the oven for 45 minutes, then turn everything over, gently. Sprinkle over the olives and dot the feta around. Roast for another 15 minutes. The feta should be soft and creamy and everything else should be on the verge of charring, but nicely soft on the bottom.

Serve immediately, sprinkled with oregano and parsley, direct from the tin, or you can remove everything to a serving platter and squish the garlic cloves into the tin juices to pour over.

Dal with Lemon or Lime Curry

Serves 4

For the dal

1 tbsp coconut oil

1 onion, finely chopped

200g/7oz sweet potato or squash, finely diced

2 garlic cloves, finely chopped

2cm/¾-in piece of fresh root ginger, peeled and finely chopped

2 tbsp finely chopped coriander (cilantro) stems (save the leaves for serving)

1 tsp ground cardamom

1 tsp ground turmeric

½ tsp ground cumin

½ tsp ground coriander

¼ tsp ground cinnamon

A pinch of ground cloves

300g/1½ cups mung beans (moong dal)

1 x 400ml tin/1¾ cups coconut milk

500ml/generous 2 cups water

Juice of 1 lemon or lime

Sea salt and freshly ground black pepper

Coriander (cilantro) leaves, to serve

I love this combination, not least because compartmentalizing flavours as I've done here can be very useful when feeding a family – children not yet able to handle the hot and sour flavours of the lemon curry will be happy with the sweet and mild spices of the dal.

Giving the option of using lemons or limes for the curry pays lip service to the fact that very few people outside the US and the UK distinguish between them. Regardless, the results will be sour and you can make it as hot as you like.

Serve with basmati rice or with some paratha, with perhaps some lightly steamed greens on the side.

Heat the coconut oil in a large saucepan or flameproof casserole. Add the onion and sauté for several minutes until starting to soften. Add the sweet potato or squash, garlic and ginger, and cook for a few more minutes. Add the coriander (cilantro) stems and all the spices, then stir in the mung beans. Pour in the coconut milk and water, then bring to the boil. Season generously with salt and pepper. Simmer, covered, until the mung beans are tender, keeping an eye on it as you don't want it to get too dry. Before serving add the lemon or lime juice and sprinkle with coriander leaves.

continued…

continued…

4 lemons or 6 limes

1 tbsp coconut oil

1 tsp cumin seeds

1 tsp mustard seeds

1 tsp coriander seeds

A few curry leaves

¼ fresh coconut, grated

1 large onion, finely chopped

5cm/2-in piece of fresh root ginger, peeled and grated

4 garlic cloves, crushed

1 tsp ground turmeric

2 tsp Kashmiri chilli powder

500ml/generous 2 cups water

1 tbsp jaggery or soft light brown sugar

For the Lemon or Lime Curry

Top and tail and lemons or limes, then cut (with peel) into 1cm/½-in dice. Put the lemons or limes in a saucepan and cover with water. Bring to the boil and simmer for 5 minutes. Drain thoroughly.

Melt the coconut oil in a saucepan or flameproof casserole. Add the whole spices with the curry leaves and fry until the mustard seeds start popping. Add the grated coconut and fry for a few minutes until it is looking lightly toasted, then add the onion, ginger and garlic. Continue to cook for a few minutes, then add the turmeric and chilli powder.

Add the lemons or limes along with the water and the jaggery. Simmer until the lemons or limes are tender and the sauce is well reduced – it should retain its light, bright yellow. Add a splash more water if you think it needs it.

Sides

There are several dishes in this chapter that I could happily eat on their own, but there is no doubt they are all useful as side dishes. I use them mainly when I want a hint of citrus in a meal but I don't want it to dominate – so most of these will be served alongside anything simply grilled, traditionally roasted, or even casseroled, as long as the accompanying sauce isn't overwhelmingly citrus. Of course, sometimes citrus dishes can complement one another – for example, I would be very comfortable serving any lemony, buttery vegetables alongside a lemon- or bergamot-scented roast chicken. Likewise the fragrant Lime and Coconut Rice (see page 145) is the perfect accompaniment to anything with sharp and sour elements.

Brussels Sprouts with Lime, Chilli and Nigella Seeds

Serves 4

500g/1lb 2oz Brussels sprouts, trimmed and halved

1 tbsp olive oil

1 tsp chipotle paste

1 garlic clove, finely chopped

Finely grated zest and juice of 1 lime

1 tsp nigella seeds

Sea salt and freshly ground black pepper

The flavours in this dish are based on a recipe in Jennifer McLagan's book *Bitter*, which is rich pickings for anyone interested in citrus fruit. If you aren't keen on Brussels sprouts or they are out of season, you could use any leafy greens in this recipe as long as they are the sort that hold their shape – no wilting spinach please.

Blanch the sprouts in plenty of boiling, salted water for 2 minutes, then drain. Heat the olive oil in a lidded frying pan and add the sprouts. Cover and cook over a medium heat, shaking the pan regularly, for 4–5 minutes, until starting to brown. Mix the chipotle with a little water and add to the pan with the garlic. Toss to coat the sprouts in the chilli, then sprinkle over the lime zest and juice along with a generous amount of salt and pepper and the nigella seeds. Cook for a further couple of minutes, then remove from the heat.

Fennel and Lemon Dauphinoise

Serves 4

A slice of butter, plus extra for greasing

2 fennel bulbs

1 lemon

300ml/1¼ cups whipping (heavy) cream

50ml/3½ tbsp milk

1 tsp plain (all-purpose) flour

3 tbsp breadcrumbs

3 tbsp roughly grated Pecorino

A grating of nutmeg

Sea salt and freshly ground black pepper

The lemon in this recipe melds seamlessly with the fennel and cream despite being unpeeled – you will get the odd burst of sour, but it never feels *de trop*. This is a perfect side dish for any simply grilled fish or meat.

Preheat the oven to 180°C/350°F/Gas mark 4. Rub a gratin dish with butter. Bring 2 saucepans of water to the boil.

Trim off and reserve any leafy fronds from the fennel, then trim the base, removing the bare minimum as you want the fennel to hold together at the roots. Finely slice lengthways. Top and tail the lemon, then slice as finely as you can, preferably with a mandoline. Add the fennel and lemon to separate saucepans of boiling water and blanch – the fennel for 3–4 minutes, the lemon for 1 minute only. Drain both.

Arrange the fennel and lemon in the gratin dish, seasoning the layers with salt and pepper as you go. In a bowl, whisk the cream with the milk and flour (just to combine, you do not want it to thicken). Pour this mixture over the fennel and lemon.

Finely chop the reserved fennel fronds and mix with the breadcrumbs and cheese. Grate in some nutmeg (a few rasps will be enough), then stir and sprinkle over the gratin. Dice the butter and dot it over the gratin. Bake in the oven for around 1 hour until the fennel and lemon are tender and the top is crisp and golden brown.

Caramelized Potatoes with Orange

Serves 4

1kg/2lb 3oz small new potatoes, scrubbed but unpeeled

100g/½ cup caster (superfine) sugar

75g/⅓ cup butter

Finely grated zest of ½ sour orange and juice of 2 sour oranges (or zest of ½ orange and ½ lime, juice of 1 orange and 1 lime)

Sea salt

The idea of caramelized potatoes is a Scandinavian one, but the addition of orange is all mine. Slathering potatoes in butter and sugar is clearly not something you want to do every day – the Scandinavians serve it as part of Christmas dinner – but is worth having as part of the repertoire to complement rich, earthy casseroles. I like to serve them with a red-wine beef or venison casserole flavoured with juniper.

It is traditional to peel the potatoes after boiling them and the caramel does stick to them better that way – but you can leave them unpeeled if you prefer; it won't make too much of a difference.

Put the potatoes in a saucepan and cover with water. Bring to the boil and add salt. Simmer until knife-tender, around 12–15 minutes. Drain and cool under running water, then peel them, if you like – you should find that the skins slip off very easily.

Melt the sugar in a large, heavy-based frying pan over a medium heat. Leave it alone, perhaps just giving it a shake every so often, until it has caramelized – it will start around the edges and eventually turn a light golden brown. Add the butter (be careful, it may splutter) and allow it to melt into the caramel, keeping the stirring to a minimum. Whisk in the zest, juice and a pinch of salt. Add the potatoes then leave to cook, slowly, and turning regularly, until the caramel has reduced down and the potatoes are well coated.

Sweet Potatoes

I love sweet potatoes with citrus as the sour/bitter does a great job of balancing what can sometimes be a slightly cloying sweetness. I think they deserve the three-way approach here; they're very good for us, after all.

Serves 4

1 garlic clove, finely chopped

Finely grated zest of 2 clementines or mandarins and juice of 4

Juice of 1 lime

1 tsp sugar or runny honey

2 sweet potatoes, preferably white, peeled and cut into chunks

1 red chilli, julienned

A few chives, finely snipped

Sea salt

Sweet Potatoes Glazed with Clementines or Mandarins

This is based on a Peruvian way of cooking sweet potatoes, although rather than the orange-fleshed variety, for this particular recipe I prefer the purple-skinned, white-fleshed sort, as they aren't quite as sweet and have a nuttier flavour that works better with the sweet clementines or mandarins. For a hint of spice, add some allspice berries or star anise to the syrup if you like.

Put the garlic, clementine or mandarin zest and juice and half the lime juice into a wide saucepan or frying pan. Add the sugar or honey and cook on a low heat, stirring until the sugar or honey has dissolved. Bring to the boil and cook down until the mixture is very lightly syrupy – you don't want it too dense. Remove from the heat and season with salt.

Meanwhile, toss the sweet potatoes in the remaining lime juice and season with salt. Steam over boiling water for 6–7 minutes. Transfer to the frying pan and very gently turn over in the syrup. Garnish with the red chilli and the chives.

Serves 4

1 tsp yuzu powder or
   freeze-dried yuzu

1 tbsp yuzu juice

½ tsp garlic powder

50g/3½ tbsp butter, well softened

4 sweet potatoes, well scrubbed

Olive oil

Sea salt

Baked Sweet Potatoes with Yuzu Butter

There isn't much yuzu juice added to this as a little goes such a long way. The garlic just rounds out the flavour a bit.

First make the yuzu butter. Beat the yuzu powder and juice, the garlic powder and ½ tsp sea salt into the butter until it is well mixed. Scoop into a container and refrigerate until you need it.

Preheat the oven to 200°C/400°F/Gas mark 6. Prick the sweet potatoes all over with a fork or knife tip, then rub with olive oil. Sprinkle with salt.

Place the sweet potatoes on a baking tray and cook for around an hour, less if they are particularly small. Slice the top down the middle, lengthways, and wait for the steam to subside. Put around a tablespoon of the butter into each cut, and serve.

Serves 4

2–3 sweet potatoes

25g/1½ tbsp butter

Finely grated zest of 2 lemons or limes
   or 1 tbsp finely chopped preserved
   lemon or lime

A small bunch of coriander (cilantro),
   finely chopped

A pinch of ground cumin

A pinch of ground coriander

A pinch of ground cardamom

Sea salt

Sweet Potato Mash with Lemon and Coriander

I have given three options on the citrus here and I love all three. The lemon zest will give a sweeter, fragrant hit of citrus, the limes (depending on type) may be slightly sourer but equally fragrant, and the preserved citrus much more of a dominant presence, giving a salty, sour note that balances well with the sweet potato. Take your pick!

There are several ways to cook sweet potatoes before mashing them. The quickest method – boiling – is not the best as it can waterlog delicate sweet potatoes. So either peel and cut into chunks then steam for 7–8 minutes (2 minutes in a pressure cooker) or – and this is my preferred method when I am not short of time – pierce the skins all over with a fork and bake in a 200°C/400°F/Gas mark 6 oven for 45 minutes to 1 hour. Cut open, let all the steam escape, then scrape out the flesh.

Whichever method you use, mash the flesh with the butter and the remaining ingredients, along with plenty of salt.

Chicory Braised with Grapefruit, Mandarin and Soy

Serves 4

1 tbsp olive oil

1 tbsp runny honey

4 heads of chicory (endive), cut in half lengthways

50g/3½ tbsp butter

Finely grated zest of 1 mandarin and 50ml/3½ tbsp juice

1 tsp finely grated grapefruit zest and 50ml/3½ tbsp juice

30ml/2 tbsp dark soy sauce

A few sprigs of thyme

Sea salt and freshly ground black pepper

This dish is heaven for anyone who loves bitter flavours – it is layering bitter on bitter, but it is slightly tempered with the mandarin juice, honey and butter. I confess I can easily eat the lot in one sitting.

It is best served alongside some grilled meat – perhaps a fatty pork steak or a thick slice of gammon. Or eat it as a supper dish with some mashed potato or bread for mopping.

Heat the olive oil in a large frying pan. Melt the honey in a small saucepan then brush over the cut edges of the chicory (endive). Sear the chicory in the frying pan, cut side down, until it has started to caramelize, then flip over and cook for a couple more minutes. Add the butter, citrus zests and juices and the soy sauce, pouring them around the chicory, then sprinkle in the thyme sprigs and season with salt and pepper. Simmer, turning regularly, until the chicory is glossy and tender, and the liquids have reduced to a syrup.

Roast Tomatoes with Lemon
and Lemon Thyme

**I can't remember what led me to this idea, but I'm so glad I tried it.
I had always been a bit either/or with tomatoes and lemons but this is a
revelation – the lemon sweetens and caramelizes in a very different way
from the tomatoes and they complement one another perfectly. These are
wonderful with grilled fish or steak, or just folded through some pasta.**

Take 400g/14oz small to medium (i.e. slightly larger than cherry) vine
tomatoes. Separate them from the vine but leave the core leaves. Heat a heavy-
based frying pan to as hot as you can get it. Add 1 tbsp olive oil and the
tomatoes. Cook, shaking regularly, until the tomatoes are threatening – but
not quite ready – to burst out of their skins. This won't take long. Cut the
peel off a large lemon (see page 15) and dice the flesh, taking out any pips as
you go. Add this into the pan – it should sizzle and start caramelizing almost
immediately. Shake a couple of times and remove. Serve sprinkled with salt
and lemon thyme, and perhaps some shredded basil if you like. Capers are
also a good addition here; you can add them just before the lemon so they
can sizzle for a moment on their own first.

Lemon, Mustard and Rosemary Potatoes

This is also good with the sweetness of celeriac. I use new or waxy potatoes here, but you could use the floury sort if you prefer.

Preheat the oven to 200°C/400°F/Gas mark 6. Scrub 1kg/2lb 3oz new potatoes and cut in half if particularly large. Thickly slice 1 onion. Whisk 100g/⅓ cup wholegrain Dijon mustard with 3 tbsp olive oil, the finely grated zest and juice of 1 lemon and plenty of salt and pepper. Toss the potatoes in this mix. Sprinkle the onion over the base of a large roasting tin then top with the potatoes. Sprinkle over lots of freshly cut rosemary. Roast in the oven, turning everything over a couple of times, for around 45–50 minutes, until the potatoes are crisp, and tender inside.

Buttered Courgettes with Lemon and Nutmeg

As much as I love grilled, charred courgettes (zucchini) with bite, I love these creamy, buttery ones more. The lemon serves to lift the dish and the nutmeg gives it almost a nursery feel. You can do this with most green vegetables: try chard, sweating the stems down until softened before you add the shredded leaves, or finely sliced runner beans – with the latter, you might want to take out the nutmeg and replace with some lightly toasted almonds.

Take 500g/1lb 2oz small, firm courgettes (zucchini) – the sort that haven't swelled from an excess of watering. Melt 30g/2 tbsp butter in a large, lidded frying pan and add the courgettes with the finely grated zest of 1 lemon and a generous amount of seasoning. Add a splash of water, then cover and braise gently for 5 minutes, stirring every so often. Remove the lid – if there seems as though there is a lot of water in the pan (there may be if you are using large courgettes), simmer until it has reduced. Add a fine rasp of nutmeg and a squeeze of lemon juice, then stir in a handful of basil just before serving.

Stir-fried Cucumbers with Orange and Szechuan Peppercorns

These cucumbers are best eaten at room temperature or even chilled down, as there is something so good about the still firm, cooling flesh with the mouth-numbing peppercorns and orange. I do usually make this with cucumbers, but also love it with the pear-shaped chayote, or christophene – an underused vegetable, which is a shame, as it is a great flavour carrier that retains a firm, smooth texture once cooked.

Take 2 large cucumbers, then peel, halve lengthways, deseed and roughly chop. Heat 1 tbsp oil in a wok. Lightly crush 1 tsp each of Szechuan peppercorns and coriander seeds and add to the wok along with 1 finely sliced chilli, a 1cm/⅜-in piece of root ginger, finely chopped, and 1 scant tsp finely grated orange zest. Stir fry for a minute, then add the cucumber along with the juice of 2 oranges. Season with salt and pepper (or simply add a dash of soy sauce), then leave to simmer for a few minutes until the orange juice has reduced to a very light syrup.

Broad Beans with Lemon and Dill

This recipe is very adaptable. I have on occasion made a double amount (I always have frozen broad (fava) beans to hand), chilled the leftovers, and mixed with sliced, grilled artichokes the next day for a quick salad. In summer, you could try using summer savory in place of the dill.

Take around 500g/4 cups baby broad (fava) beans – when small they don't really need their skins removed. If you are using larger beans, increase the amount to 600g/4¾ cups and skin them. Slice 1 shallot very finely and sauté in 1 tbsp olive oil and 10g/2 tsp butter. Add the beans with the finely grated zest of 1 lemon, plenty of seasoning and a splash of water. Cover and braise for 4–5 minutes until tender. Taste and squeeze in plenty of lemon juice, then stir in lots of freshly cut dill.

Citrus and Rice

There are endless possibilities when combining citrus with rice, and you can adapt any of these recipes to your favourite type. In particular, I love a sticky black rice scented with lime, or a wild rice with lots of orange notes. These are side dishes in which the role of citrus is to scent gently and add more background flavour, and, as it's more about subtlety than big impact flavours, I use pieces of pared zest that can be fished out at the end of cooking, rather than a fine grating.

These recipes incorporate citrus from the start, but it is worth pointing out that you can also dress cooked rice for a quick side dish or main leftover meal – a yuzu ponzu, some leftover sauce (try the sauce from the Seville Orange-Spiced Duck, page 110), or any salad dressing is excellent with leftover steamed rice.

Gently Scented Rice

For this fragrant, mellow dish, use pared lemon or lime zest, or leaves – anything else will be too bitter. Rinse 300g/1¾ cups of your choice of rice – basmati or jasmine work best – under plenty of cold water until it is running clear. Drain thoroughly and add to a saucepan with a generous pinch of salt and either a few pieces of pared lemon, lime or mandarin zest or a handful of citrus leaves. Add any other aromatics you like, then add 450ml/1¾ cups freshly boiled water, or a light stock. Return to the boil, then turn down and cover, putting a tea towel or a few sheets of kitchen paper between the pot and its lid. Simmer until all the liquid has been absorbed, around 15 minutes, then remove from the heat and leave to steam for a further 5–10 minutes. You should have perfectly dry, fluffy, aromatic rice.

Bitter Orange Rice

Essentially a pilau, this recipe relies on dried pared citrus peel. It is based on a Middle Eastern way with bitter orange and rice – the zest has to be blanched otherwise it imparts a far too bitter flavour. You can use any bitter-skinned citrus here as long as you blanch it thoroughly first. You can buy the dried, shredded peel of bitter oranges – if using this sort, still blanch, but tie into muslin before adding to the rice, so it can be easily removed.

Put a few pieces of dried bitter orange peel in a saucepan and cover with water. Bring to the boil and simmer for 5 minutes, then drain and rinse. Repeat this twice more. Follow the instructions for Gently Scented Rice (see opposite), adding any aromatics you like – I will usually include a bay leaf, a few cardamom pods, a small piece of cinnamon, a few peppercorns and coriander seeds. Rinse 500g/3 cups basmati rice as before. Fry the spices and orange peel in 1 tbsp oil, then add the rice. For an even sweeter touch, add 50g/⅓ cup finely chopped dates as well. Stir to coat, then pour in 750ml/3 cups freshly boiled water. Cook as before – after 15 minutes, push holes in the rice with a wooden spoon handle, top with slices of butter and sprinkle with a few drops of orange blossom water. Leave to stand, covered, for another 10 minutes.

Lime and Coconut Rice

This includes finely grated zest and I use it mainly with Caribbean style dishes – but if you want to make it more Thai, you can add a bruised lemongrass stem and just 1 small kaffir lime leaf as well. Rinse 300g/1¾ cups rice as for Gently Scented Rice (see opposite), and put in a saucepan. Season and add the finely grated zest and juice of 1 lime. Sprinkle over 50g/1¾oz powdered coconut milk (the sort you usually rehydrate before use, not coconut flour) and add 450ml/1¾ cups boiling water. Cook as for the Gently Scented Rice, making sure you remove from the heat and leave to steam for at least 10 minutes at the end. Garnish with coriander (cilantro) and some freshly shaved coconut if you like. I will sometimes add 200g/1 cup cooked black beans to this as well, although the colour will obviously suffer for it. This is very good with the Mojo Chicken on page 109.

Roasted Cauliflower with Lemon, Nigella Seeds and Gremolata

Gremolata is a very useful thing to know how to make quickly as most people will usually have some kind of citrus zest, garlic and soft herb in the house. I use coriander (cilantro) here as this recipe has Asian notes to it, but it is more traditional to use parsley. You can also use preserved citrus instead of fresh zest. You can sprinkle this gremolata over any meaty casserole, or turn into a dressing for grilled chicken or fish, as suggested below.

Preheat the oven to 200°C/400°F/Gas mark 6. Break a large cauliflower into florets and cut the larger florets in half lengthways. Break up a head of garlic and leave the cloves unpeeled. Add both to a roasting tin. Mix together 1 tbsp olive oil with the juice of 1 lemon or lime (finely grate the zest before juicing, and reserve). Add salt, 1 tsp nigella seeds, ½ tsp cumin seeds and ½ tsp dried chilli flakes (red pepper flakes), or you can use a finely chopped fresh chilli instead if you prefer. Pour this over the cauliflower and garlic, turn to coat then spread out into an even layer. Roast for around 35–40 minutes until the cauliflower is nicely charred and al dente.

To make the gremolata, finely chop 2 garlic cloves and a small bunch of coriander (cilantro). Mix together with the reserved lemon or lime zest and season with salt. This can also be turned into a type of dressing with more olive oil and citrus juice if you prefer. Serve separately at the table.

Desserts

It was only when thinking about all the sweeter uses of citrus – whether in desserts, drinks, preserves and sweets – that I was struck by something I now see as obvious: I do not ever remember seeing fresh limes as a child. I do realize now that during my childhood my love of citrus desserts was quite polarized. On the one hand, I loved the "first principles" cooking of my mother – fresh lemons and oranges used in mousses, steamed puddings, ice creams, and her famous Blood Orange and Rhubarb Meringue Pie (see page 150). Only very occasionally did we have Jif lemon juice – perhaps to accompany the sugar she whizzed up in a cracked coffee grinder to serve with pancakes on Shrove Tuesday. On the other hand, my paternal grandmother gave me a love of highly processed limes – Rowntree's lime jelly, broken up with evaporated milk, limeade (her remedy for any stomach ailments), chocolate limes. I find myself nostalgic for all of these things, despite knowing I do not now enjoy them. The desserts that have stuck with me come from my mother's kitchen. She didn't pander to us children by diluting the sour/bitter flavours and sometimes it was a bit much – a honey and lemon steamed pudding made with lemon slices was too sharp and a bit chewy, and a marmalade steamed pudding too bitter. But I find myself doing the same with my own children and I fare better.

I have included favourite dishes, old and new, in this section, but there are so many very simple ideas that can serve as impromptu, last-minute desserts and breakfasts. For example, infusing pared zest or citrus leaves in milk or cream will make the best custards, ice creams, rice puddings. Pancakes are always best just with lemon and sugar, but try other citrus (as long as there is acidity) or use syrups adulterated with a small amount of citrus-based alcohol. Dig out your curved, serrated grapefruit knife and update the classic grapefruit half, sprinkled with demerara sugar and brûléed; perhaps add a few drops of bitters too. Above all, don't forget the transformative powers of citrus over other fruits. I can't imagine papaya without a squeeze of lime; try adding it to mango, watermelon, strawberries and bananas. Grilled pineapple or bananas will always benefit from a squeeze of lime and a dash of rum. Oranges have an affinity with strawberries and raspberries, lemons with blackberries. Just remember that when it comes to making fruit salads, less is more – stick to a main fruit, a citrus and perhaps another spicy herbal note (basil with orange and strawberries, mint with lime and watermelon) and you won't go far wrong.

Rum and Orange
Bread and Butter Pudding

Serves 6

Butter, for greasing and spreading

50g/⅓ cup raisins

Pared zest of 1 lime or ½ Seville orange

75ml/5 tbsp dark rum

6 large slices of brioche, panettone or
  pandoro

Lime or orange curd (see page 224 for
  homemade), for spreading

Nutmeg, for grating

4 eggs

25g/2 tbsp caster (superfine) sugar

500ml/2 cups plus 1 tbsp whole milk

2 tbsp demerara sugar

Many popular desserts in the Caribbean are based on classic European favourites, and this is no exception. Brioche or panettone are often used, along with rum-infused raisins and an orange or lime curd. You could substitute with marmalade if you like.

Preheat the oven to 180°C/350°F/Gas mark 3. Butter a 1.5-litre/3-pint oven dish.

Put the raisins and citrus zest in a small saucepan and pour in the rum. Bring to the boil then immediately remove from the heat and leave to infuse.

Spread each slice of bread with butter and a thick layer of curd, then cut each slice into 4 triangles. Arrange a layer of the triangles in the dish, butter and curd side up. Strain the raisins, reserving the rum, and sprinkle over two thirds of the raisins. Grate over a little nutmeg then layer the remaining bread slices over the top.

Whisk the eggs together in a jug, then beat in the caster (superfine) sugar and milk. Add the reserved rum. Pour this mixture over the bread, slowly and carefully – a torrent of liquid will dislodge the bread and make it float out of place.

Sprinkle over the remaining raisins and the demerara sugar, then add a few more rasps of nutmeg. Leave to stand for at least 10 minutes to allow the custard to soak thoroughly into the bread, then bake in the oven for 30–40 minutes until golden brown with slightly caramelized patches from the sugar, butter and curd. Serve with pouring cream.

Blood Orange and Rhubarb Meringue Pie

Serves 6

For the pastry

225g/1¾ cups plain (all-purpose) flour, plus extra for dusting

150g/⅔ cup butter, chilled and diced

1 egg yolk

A pinch of salt

For the filling

400g/14oz rhubarb, preferably the pink forced kind, cut into short (2cm/¾-in) lengths

60g/⅓ cup caster (superfine) sugar

Finely grated zest of 2 blood oranges and juice of up to 4 blood oranges

1 tbsp cornflour (cornstarch)

3 egg yolks

30g/1 tbsp butter (optional)

For the meringue topping

4 egg whites (left from pastry and filling)

225g/1¼ cups caster (superfine) sugar

½ tsp cream of tartar

Most meringue pies use a sweet pastry, but as I find the meringue so sweet, I think it is better served with a very buttery shortcrust (pie dough), so I take out the sugar. The butter in the filling is optional – it's not always used and I think it adds a richness, making the filling more like curd and less like custard.

First make the pastry. Either whiz the flour and butter in a food processor or rub in by hand until the mixture resembles fine breadcrumbs, then add the egg yolk and salt. Mix briefly, adding a little chilled water if necessary, until you can bring the pastry together into a ball – it should need no more than a tablespoon. Wrap in plastic wrap and chill for at least 30 minutes in the refrigerator. Preheat the oven to 190°C/375°F/Gas mark 5.

Roll out the pastry on a lightly floured work surface and use to line a pie dish (between 21 and 23cm/8¼ and 9-in diameter). Prick all over with a fork, then line with baking parchment and fill with baking beans. Bake for 20 minutes, then remove the beans and bake for a further 5 minutes or so until the pastry is a light golden brown. Remove from the oven.

To make the filling, put the rhubarb into a baking dish, sprinkle with the sugar and orange zest and roast in the oven for 30–35 minutes, stirring every so often – if you are organized you can cook this at the same time as you are blind baking the pastry. Strain the rhubarb juice into a measuring jug and set aside the solids. Add enough blood orange juice to make up the rhubarb juice to 250ml/1 cup plus 1 tbsp. Use a small amount of the liquid to whisk the cornflour (cornstarch) into a thin paste in a bowl, and heat the rest in a medium saucepan. When the liquid is hot, pour some of it over the cornflour mixture, whisking

continued...

continued…

constantly, then pour this back into the saucepan. Stir over a low heat until the mixture thickens – this is likely to happen very suddenly. Add the egg yolks and butter, if using, and continue to whisk. Remove from the heat and stir through the reserved rhubarb. Pour into the cooked pastry case. If you have time, leave it to cool and chill down completely as it will help the texture enormously and prevent possible separation.

To make the meringue, whisk the egg whites in a large bowl until well aerated and just starting to form stiff peaks. Continuing to whisk, add the sugar a tablespoon at a time until the meringue is beautifully stiff and glossy, then add the remaining sugar all at once, and sprinkle in the cream of tartar. Pipe or pile the meringue over the filling.

Bake in the oven for around 15–20 minutes until the meringue is a dappled golden brown. I love this both hot and cold and I don't think it needs any embellishment.

Chocolate Lime Puddings

Serves 8

For the chocolate pudding

200g/¾ cup plus 2 tbsp butter, plus
  an extra 1 tbsp, melted, for greasing

200g/7oz dark chocolate, broken
  into pieces

2 tbsp rum

100g/½ cup caster (superfine) sugar

4 eggs, plus 4 egg yolks

60g/7¼ tbsp plain (all-purpose) flour

8 candied limequats

For the lime syrup

100g/½ cup caster (superfine) sugar

Finely grated zest of 3 limes

100ml/7 tbsp lime juice

A pinch of salt

2 tbsp white rum or tequila (optional)

Note

**If you haven't any candied
limequats, don't worry – just miss
them out as this pudding is superb
with just the lime syrup.**

**On my list of favourite childhood sweets are chocolate
limes – suck your way through a hard candy lime shell
and you suddenly hit the chocolate within. This is a
dessert version, based on a classic chocolate fondant.**

Preheat the oven to 200°C/400°F/Gas mark 6. Brush the
insides of 8 small pudding basins with the melted butter.

Put the chocolate, butter and rum in a saucepan and melt
together over a very low heat. If you are nervous about doing
this over a direct flame, you can instead put everything in a
bowl and place it over a simmering saucepan of water. The
butter will melt first and at this stage you can remove it
from the heat as it should be hot enough to melt the rest
of the chocolate. Stir thoroughly and allow to cool slightly.

Put the sugar, whole eggs and egg yolks into a large bowl
and whisk until the mixture has reached the ribbon stage –
it should be at least doubled in volume, very aerated, and
when you drizzle a line of the mixture across the surface it
should take a while to melt back into the whole.

Pour the chocolate and butter mixture into the egg mixture
gradually, then sift over the flour. Stir everything together,
slowly and gently, until the mixture is fully combined and a
rich dark ochre.

Put a heaped tablespoon of mixture in each of the pudding
basins, then rest a candied limequat in the centre. Divide
the rest of the mixture between the basins. Place on a baking
tray and bake for around 10–12 minutes. When cooked, the
top should be springy to touch and they should have very
slightly shrunk away from the sides.

Meanwhile, make the lime syrup. Put the sugar, lime zest and
juice into a small saucepan and heat until the sugar has melted.
Simmer for a few minutes until syrupy then add the salt and
alcohol. Simmer for another minute and decant to a jug.

To serve the puddings, run a palette knife around the edge
of each basin and upturn onto a serving plate or bowl. Pour
over the syrup at the table and serve with whipping (heavy)
cream too, if you like.

Blackberry and Lemon Steamed Pudding with Lemon and Gin Sauce

Serves 4–6

75g/⅓ cup butter, softened, plus
   extra for greasing

135g/¾ cup caster (superfine) sugar

1 tbsp cornflour (cornstarch)

200g/1½ cups blackberries

100g/¾ cup self-raising (self-rising)
   flour

2 large eggs

Finely grated zest and juice of 1 lemon

1–2 tbsp milk (if needed)

For the sauce

Finely grated zest and juice of
   1 large lemon

50g/¼ cup caster (superfine) sugar

100ml/7 tbsp water

50ml/3½ tbsp gin

Every year I find myself playing a game of cat and mouse with the scent of blackberries – it is one of my favourite smells yet it is so elusive. Happily, the addition of lemon in this pudding really helps to define it, in much the same way Bramley apples do. The sauce is a Jane Grigson classic that I find has a great affinity with the blackberries.

Grease a 1.5-litre/3-pint pudding basin generously with butter. Put 50g/4 tbsp of the caster (superfine) sugar and the cornflour (cornstarch) into a bowl and mix to combine and get rid of any lumps. Add the blackberries and toss so they are thoroughly coated. Put these in the base of the buttered pudding basin.

Put the butter, remaining sugar, flour, eggs and lemon zest and juice in a food processor or mixer and blitz until you have a smooth batter. Aim for a dropping consistency and add the milk if necessary.

Pour the batter over the blackberries, making sure the blackberries don't push through round the edges. Fold a pleat into a square of foil and cover the top of the basin, tying it into place with string or fastening with a fat rubber band.

Steam for around 2 hours over a simmering saucepan of water – or in a pressure cooker for 35 minutes, making sure the first 20 minutes isn't at pressure.

To make the sauce, put the zest, sugar and water in a small saucepan. Stir on a low heat until the sugar is completely dissolved, then cover and leave to simmer for 20 minutes – this will give the lemon a chance to infuse and the liquid to become syrupy. Add the lemon juice and gin, then immediately strain into a serving jug.

To serve, remove the lid from the pudding and lightly run a palette knife around the edge. Put a serving plate over the pudding basin and flip over so the pudding drops onto the plate. Serve with the sauce and plenty of cream.

Sussex Pond Puddings

Serves 8

25g/1½ tbsp butter, plus extra for greasing

200g/1½ cups self-raising (self-rising) flour, plus extra for dusting

A pinch of salt

75g/2½oz suet

About 150ml/10 tbsp milk

For the filling

150g/⅔ cup butter

150g/¾ cup demerara sugar

3 pieces of stem ginger, finely chopped

8 kumquats or limequats

Variation

If you would like to make the classic Sussex pond pudding, use the same amount of suet pastry to line a 2-litre/3½ pint basin. Use all the butter and sugar in the same way, omitting the stem ginger, and use 1 whole lemon, orange or perhaps a couple of limes, making sure you pierce them thoroughly all over with a skewer. Steam for 3½–4 hours.

This pudding is the exception to my rule that kumquats are only worth bothering with if candied, as they infuse beautifully with the sugar and butter in this recipe, which gives a similar effect. Suet puddings are celebrated by the British and viewed with suspicion by everyone else – I love them and have found them infinitely adaptable (see variation, below).

Incidentally, this quantity of suet pastry can be put to good use in other citrusy ways. Try rolling it out into a large rectangle and filling with marmalade for a roly poly.

Generously butter 8 individual-sized pudding basins and set aside. Put the flour and salt into a bowl, then rub in the suet and butter. Gradually add the milk, cutting it in with a knife until you have a fairly soft, but roll-able dough. Knead lightly to make sure it is well combined (it will not be very smooth because of the suet) and not sticky, then turn out onto a floured surface. Divide the mixture into 8 – the easiest way to do this is by weighing it and dividing accordingly. Roll each piece of dough into a round, then cut a quarter out of it. Use each larger piece of the circle to line the pudding basins.

Cut up the butter for the filling into small squares and divide half of it between the 8 basins. Follow with half the demerara sugar and stem ginger. Stand the kumquats or limequats upright in the centre of the butter and sugar. Cover with the rest of the butter, sugar and ginger. Form the remaining pieces dough into rounds and use to cover the puddings, making sure you seal the edges together.

Cover each of the puddings with pleated foil and tie firmly around the rim – if you have a supply of rubber bands, these are the easiest thing to use. Steam for around 2 hours until golden brown. When you are ready to serve, turn out and serve with pouring cream or crème anglaise.

Shaker Lemon Pie

Serves 6–8

For the filling

2 large or 3 small lemons

450g/2½ cups golden caster (superfine) sugar

A pinch of salt

4 eggs

60g/¼ cup butter, melted

50g/6 tbsp plain (all-purpose) flour, plus extra for dusting

For the pastry

65g/¼ cup plus 1 tsp butter, well chilled and diced

65g/¼ cup plus 1 tsp lard, well chilled and diced

250g/1¾ cups plus 2 tbsp spelt or plain (all-purpose) flour

A little milk, for brushing

My expectations weren't high when I first made this pie; I thought it owed its existence to parsimony – the whole lemon is used – and it is frequently made with sweeter Meyer lemons. However, I found it was wonderful when made with decent Italian lemons. Attempt this only if you have a mandoline or a hand steady enough to slice the lemons to a translucent, razor thinness, otherwise the lemon skin may be chewy.

You will need to start this a day before you want to bake it. Wash and dry the lemons, then slice as thinly as you possibly can, preferably with a mandoline, flicking out the seeds as you go. Put the lemon slices in a bowl and cover with the sugar and salt. Stir thoroughly, then cover and leave to macerate for at least 24 hours.

The next day start by making the pastry. Either rub the fats into the spelt flour, or pulse in a food processor until you have a consistency of fine breadcrumbs. Add chilled water sparingly until you can form a smooth dough. Form into a ball then cut into two pieces, one slightly larger than the other. Wrap in plastic wrap and refrigerate for an hour.

Preheat the oven to 200°C/400°F/Gas mark 6. Roll out the larger round of the pastry on a lightly floured work surface and use it to line a pie dish (between 21 and 23cm/8¼ and 9-in diameter). Next, whisk the eggs and melted butter together, then sprinkle over the 6 tbsp flour and whisk to combine. Pour this over the macerating lemons and mix well. Pour the whole lot into the lined pie dish.

Roll out the remaining pastry and use it to cover the pie, wetting the edges and crimping together. Decorate the pie with any leftover pastry and brush with milk. Cut a couple of slits in the centre of the pie.

Bake in the oven for around 30 minutes, then reduce the temperature to 160°C/325°F/Gas mark 3 and continue to cook for another 20 minutes. Serve hot or cold. I like it hot with a big dollop of clotted cream, but a sweet custard would be just as good.

Blackberry, Orange and Orange Blossom Clafoutis

Serves 4–6

For the baking dish

30g/2 tbsp butter, softened

2 tsp dried orange zest (see page 18), ground to a powder

2 tbsp demerara sugar

For the blackberries

300g/2¼ cups blackberries

2 tbsp caster (superfine) sugar

2 tbsp crème de mûre

For the batter

50g/6 tbsp plain (all-purpose) flour

50g/¼ cup caster (superfine) sugar

A pinch of salt

200ml/¾ cup plus 1 tbsp whole milk

50ml/3½ tbsp single cream

30g/1 tbsp butter, melted

1 tsp finely grated orange zest and juice of ½ orange

1 tsp orange blossom water

2 tsp Grand Marnier, or ideally Mandarine Napoléon (optional)

2 eggs

To serve

1 tbsp icing (confectioners') sugar

1 tsp dried orange zest (see page 18), ground to a powder

Pouring cream

Two of my favourite aromas – blackberries cooking and orange blossom – make this quite a blissful dessert for me. If you can get Mandarine Napoléon, please use it instead of an orange liqueur as it is so, so much nicer.

Put the blackberries in a bowl and sprinkle over the sugar and crème de mûre. Leave to stand for an hour.

Preheat the oven to 180°C/350°F/Gas mark 4. Spread the butter over the base of a shallow ovenproof dish (between 21 and 23cm/8¼ and 9-in diameter). Mix the orange zest and demerara sugar together and sprinkle this over the butter. Make sure the dish is evenly covered.

Put the flour in a mixing bowl with the caster (superfine) sugar and salt. Give a quick whisk to get rid of any lumps. In a separate bowl, mix together the milk, cream, melted butter, orange zest and juice, orange blossom water and liqueur, if using. Make a well in the middle of the flour and sugar, then break in the eggs. Using a whisk, work in the flour, incorporating from the edge of the well, until you have a thick paste, then gradually incorporate the wet ingredients. (You can instead put everything in a food processor and blend.)

Spoon the blackberries into the prepared dish, straining them a little as you go, and making sure they are evenly spread. Pour over the batter and bake in the oven for around 25–30 minutes until slightly puffed up and a light golden brown – it should still be slightly wobbly in the middle.

Mix the icing (confectioners') sugar and orange zest together. Let the clafoutis cool a little, then sprinkle over the sugar and zest mixture. Serve with pouring cream.

Blood Orange and Cardamom Tarte Tatin

Serves 6

2–3 blood oranges, depending on size

30ml/2 tbsp water

100g/½ cup granulated sugar

75g/⅓ cup unsalted butter, chilled
  and diced

Seeds extracted from 2 tsp cardamom
  pods, lightly crushed

300g/10½oz block of puff pastry

Plain (all-purpose) flour, for dusting

For the crème anglaise

250ml/1 cup plus 1 tbsp whole milk

250ml/1 cup plus 1 tbsp double
  (heavy) cream

1 tsp cardamom pods, lightly crushed

1 coffee bean

3cm/1¼-in piece of vanilla pod

50g/¼ cup caster (superfine) sugar

6 egg yolks

A citrus spiced tarte Tatin is proper winter comfort food, best eaten in February when blood oranges are in season and we need that hit of spice and colour to see us through. There are elements to this dish that transfer very well to other types of desserts. For example, you can exchange pastry for a sponge batter to make an upside-down cake.

If you don't want to make crème anglaise you can serve instead with Chantilly cream – just whip cream until fairly stiff and stir in a tablespoon of icing (confectioners') sugar mixed with a generous pinch of finely ground cardamom.

Preheat the oven to 180°C/350°F/Gas mark 4.

Top and tail the blood oranges, then slice very thinly. Set aside.

Put the water in the base of a 23cm/9-in cast-iron skillet or similar ovenproof pan. Sprinkle the sugar over the water in an even layer. Heat gently, resisting the urge to stir, just shaking every so often, until the sugar has melted and turned a light golden brown – you don't want it too dark at this stage. The water will help stop it browning too quickly around the edges. Remove from the heat and stir in the butter and cardamom seeds, trying not to froth it up too much.

Arrange the best orange slices in the caramel. On a lightly floured work surface, thinly roll out the pastry (to around 3mm/⅛-in), then prick all over with a fork. Cut into a round very slightly larger than your skillet, then lie it over the oranges, making sure the edges are tucked in.

continued…

continued…

Bake in the oven for around 30 minutes until the pastry is golden brown.

For the crème anglaise, put the milk and cream in a saucepan with the cardamom pods, coffee bean, vanilla and 1 tablespoon of the sugar. Bring to the boil, slowly. When on the point of boiling, remove from the heat and leave to infuse until cool.

Meanwhile, whisk the egg yolks and remaining sugar together until pale with a mousse-like consistency. Reheat the milk and cream until almost at boiling point. Pour the milk over the egg yolks and sugar in a steady stream, stirring constantly, then rinse out the pan. Pour everything back into the pan and stir on a low heat until the custard thickens – it should be thick enough to coat the back of a spoon well enough that you can draw a line through it.

Strain the custard into a jug. Serve hot or cold, but make sure you cover with plastic wrap – touching the top layer of the custard – to stop a skin from forming.

Yuzu, Mandarin and Ginger Soufflé

Serves 4–6

Softened butter, for greasing

100g/½ cup caster (superfine) sugar, plus extra for dusting

4 large eggs

Finely grated zest and juice of ½ yuzu or lemon (or 1 tsp powdered zest and 2 tbsp juice)

Finely grated zest and juice of 1 mandarin

2cm/¾-in piece of fresh root ginger, peeled and grated

Single (light) cream, to serve

This is a chilled, non-collapsing variety of soufflé, so is a good stress-free option for dessert. As fresh yuzu are very hard to come by, I often use a good-quality yuzu juice and powdered zest for this recipe.

Preheat the oven to 190°C/375°F/Gas mark 5. Brush the insides of 6 small or 4 medium ramekins with softened butter, brushing it from base to top, as this will aid rising. Dust with sugar and set aside.

Separate the eggs. Whisk the egg yolks until they are very pale, fluffy and have increased substantially in volume, then gradually whisk in half the sugar, the yuzu or lemon zest and juice, the mandarin zest and juice, and the ginger.

Whisk the egg whites in a large bowl until fairly stiff, then gradually add the remaining sugar. You want the mixture to be stiff and glossy, but not quite as dry as you would expect for meringues.

Fold a couple of tablespoons of the egg whites into the egg yolk mixture, using a metal spoon. When the mixture is slightly loosened, incorporate the rest, in three batches, trying to keep as much of the volume as possible.

Divide the mixture between the ramekins – it should reach the top. Make sure the tops of the soufflés are flat (you can do this with a palette knife), then run a finger round the rim of each.

Put the ramekins into a roasting tin. Put in the oven, then pour just-boiled water around them – it should come halfway up. Bake for 15–20 minutes, depending on the size of ramekins you have used. The soufflés should be well risen and golden brown.

These can be eaten immediately. Alternatively, cool and chill – they shouldn't collapse.

Bergamot and Rose Turkish Delight Pavlova

Serves 6–8

For the pavlova base

6 large egg whites

300g/1⅓ cups caster (superfine) sugar

1 tsp cornflour (cornstarch)

1 tsp white wine vinegar

150g/5¼oz rose and bergamot Turkish delight (see page 226), finely chopped

For the filling

500ml/generous 2 cups double (heavy) cream

25g/2¾ tbsp icing (confectioners') sugar

150g/5¼oz lemon or lemon and bergamot curd (see page 224)

1–2 tbsp limoncello or bergamot-cello (see page 248)

50g/1¾oz rose and bergamot Turkish delight (see page 226), finely diced

A few crystallized or fresh rose petals, to decorate

Variation

Stir 75g/2½oz chopped dark chocolate through the meringue in place of the Turkish delight. Combine the cream with a little orange blossom water, orange curd and a little orange liqueur, then make a quick chocolate sauce with 30g/1oz chocolate and 100ml/ 7 tbsp cream, to pour over the top.

You can make this into one, joyous, celebratory pavlova, or make individual meringues. It is of course endlessly adaptable – you can use any sort of Turkish delight or curd. Or see below for another pavlova idea.

First make the meringue base – this can be made ahead of time and kept for several days in an airtight container, or frozen. Preheat the oven to 160°C/325°F/Gas mark 3. Draw a circle the size of a dinner plate on a piece of baking parchment, for guidance, and turn the parchment upside down.

Whisk the egg whites until they have reached the soft peak stage – airy and light, but not yet very stiff and dry. Start adding the sugar, a dessertspoon at a time, whisking vigorously, until all the sugar has been incorporated and the meringue is glossy and keeps its shape. Mix the cornflour (cornstarch) and vinegar together and incorporate this, then fold in the Turkish delight.

Spoon the meringue onto the baking parchment, staying within the marked circle. Make a slight dip in the centre if you like and make sure plenty of peaks form by lightly touching the meringue with the back of a spoon and pulling it away.

Put the meringue in the oven and turn the temperature down to 140°C/275°F/Gas mark 1. Leave to bake for between 1 and 1½ hours, then turn off the oven and leave in the oven until it has cooled down. The meringue should easily peel away from the paper.

To assemble, whisk the cream with the icing (confectioners') sugar until billowy – make sure it isn't too stiff. Stir through most of the lemon curd, the limoncello or bergamot-cello and the Turkish delight, but go easy – you want a rippled effect, not homogeneity. Top with more lemon curd, Turkish delight and the rose petals.

Classic Lemon Tart

Serves 8

For the pastry

200g/1½ cups plain (all-purpose) flour, plus extra for dusting

A pinch of salt

125g/½ cup plus 1 tbsp butter, chilled and diced

50g/heaping ⅓ cup icing (confectioners') sugar

2 egg yolks

For the filling

6 eggs

300g/1½ cups plus 2 tbsp caster (superfine) sugar

250ml/1 cup plus 1 tbsp double (heavy) cream

Finely grated zest of 2 lemons and juice of 3 lemons

For the brûlée (optional)

3–4 tbsp icing (confectioners') sugar

Note

The brûléed top is entirely optional here. I do sometimes like that extra bitter hit, but just as often I don't. So don't feel obliged to invest in a blowtorch.

I've played around with the flavours in this tart a lot over the years and have come to the conclusion that although lime and Seville orange are all very well, somehow their flavours don't sing out in quite the same way as those of lemon and grapefruit. Bergamot and mandarin also work well with the lemon.

First make the pastry. Put the flour and salt into a bowl. Rub in the butter until the mixture resembles fine breadcrumbs, then stir in the icing (confectioners') sugar. Add the egg yolks and work everything together, adding a few drops of very cold water if it is too crumbly. Wrap in plastic wrap and leave to rest in the refrigerator for 30 minutes. Preheat the oven to 180°C/350°F/Gas mark 4.

On a lightly floured work surface, roll out the pastry as thinly as you can and use it to line a 23cm/9-in fluted tart tin, making sure it is pushed well into the edges (use a bit of dough to do this). Trim the edges a little, then put in the freezer for 10 minutes. Prick the pastry with a fork, then cover with baking parchment. Pour in baking beans and bake for 15 minutes. Remove the baking beans and parchment then return to the oven for a further 5 minutes. Leave to cool and turn the oven down to 150°C/300°F/Gas mark 2.

To make the filling, beat the eggs and caster (superfine) sugar together briefly using a balloon whisk, just to combine thoroughly, then add the cream, lemon zest and juice. Pour carefully into the pastry case – the easiest way to do this is to put the tart tin on a baking tray in the oven, pull out slightly, and pour directly in from a jug, so you don't have to carry it.

Bake for around 30–40 minutes until just set – it should have a slight wobble. Do not worry if it has souffléd up a little – this can sometimes happen, but it will soon deflate back down again. Leave to cool.

If you want to brûlée the tart before serving, either preheat your grill to its highest setting or use a kitchen blowtorch. Sprinkle the sugar evenly over the surface and either put under the grill or use the blowtorch – from a distance – until the sugar has melted, caramelized and set hard.

Lime, Ginger and Passionfruit
Icebox Pie

Serves 6–8

For the base

200g/7oz gingernut biscuits

½ tsp ground ginger

¼ tsp ground cinnamon

¼ tsp grated nutmeg

50g/3½ tbsp butter, melted

For the filling

150g/⅔ cup cream cheese

50ml/3½ tbsp double (heavy) cream

200g/½ cup plus 2 tbsp condensed milk

Finely grated zest of about 4 limes and 100ml/7 tbsp juice

1 egg white, beaten until stiff

To serve

250ml/1 generous cup whipping or double (heavy) cream

1 tbsp icing (confectioners') sugar

2–3 passionfruit

This cross between a no-bake cheesecake and a Key lime pie is my stepdaughter Lilly's favourite. This is lucky for me, as every Christmas we have a lot of offcuts from making gingerbread houses that end up pulverized and stored in the freezer ready to use for bases, as here. You can make little individual ones instead if you prefer.

Crush the gingernut biscuits until they resemble fine breadcrumbs, either in a food processor or by putting them in a plastic bag and bashing with a rolling pin. Put into a bowl, stir in the spices, pour over the butter, mix well, then press into a 23cm/9-in round tart tin, preferably a loose-bottomed one. Put into the freezer for a few minutes while you make the filling.

Put the cream cheese in a bowl and break up with a wooden spoon. In a separate bowl, very lightly whip the cream to soft peaks. Add the condensed milk and the lime zest and juice to the cream cheese, and beat with an electric hand-held whisk until smooth. Gently fold in the whipped cream and the beaten egg white.

Pour the mixture over the cooled ginger base, then freeze for several hours. Remove from the freezer 10 minutes before you want to serve it. Whip the cream for serving with the icing (confectioners') sugar, then pile into the centre of the pie. Drizzle over the passionfruit seeds and pulp. Serve immediately.

Lemon and Lemon Verbena
Pots de Crème

Serves 6

Pared zest of 1 lemon

A few fresh or dried lemon
  verbena leaves

240ml/1 cup water

350ml/1½ cups (heavy) whipping
  cream

6 egg yolks

100g/½ cup caster (superfine) sugar

A pinch of salt

1 tbsp lime juice

Borage flowers, to decorate (optional)

These little pots have a complex floral, almost heady flavour. How many lemon verbena (vervaine) leaves you need depends largely on the quality – some dried ones are so strong you will only need four or five. You can also use lemon balm or even lemongrass if you like. All of these flavours are subtly different from one another but will enhance the lemon, rather than obliterate it.

Serve with the little Citrus Butter Biscuits on page 191, omitting the citrus zest and blitzing a few sprigs of either rosemary or lemon thyme with the sugar before beating with the butter.

Preheat the oven to 160°C/325°F/Gas mark 3. Put the lemon zest and lemon verbena leaves in a small saucepan. Cover with the water and bring to the boil, then simmer down until the water has reduced to around 75ml/5 tbsp. Add the cream and heat gently until warm, then remove from the heat.

Meanwhile, whisk the egg yolks with the sugar and salt until very pale and mousse-like in texture – the mixture should pass the ribbon test (when you drizzle a line of the mixture across the surface it should take a while to melt back into the whole). Strain the infused cream into the egg yolks and stir to combine – at this stage do not use a whisk, because you don't want the mixture to be aerated, you need it to be a smooth, dense custard. Stir until any foam from the eggs has abated.

Divide between 6 ramekins. Put in a roasting tin and pour just-boiled water around the ramekins to come about halfway up. Cook in the oven for around 20 minutes until the custards are just set, with a slight wobble in the centre. Remove from the oven and cool down. Transfer to the refrigerator to chill, preferably overnight.

Decorate with borage flowers if you have them, and serve with little butter biscuits.

Mandarin Crème Caramel

Serves 6

For the caramel
100g/½ cup caster (superfine) sugar

For the crème
500ml/2 cups plus 1 tbsp whole milk
Finely grated zest of 2 mandarins
A pinch of anise seeds (optional)
2 eggs, plus 2 egg yolks
100g/½ cup caster (superfine) sugar

Note
Mandarin has a great affinity with aniseed notes – I love it with basil, too, for the same reason – but you can omit it if it does not appeal.

I can't think of many desserts I prefer to a proper, silky-soft, well-chilled crème caramel – apart from the Spanish version, *flan de naranja* from Valencia, which uses orange juice instead of milk. Here I still use milk but infuse it with mandarin zest and anise. The beauty of crème caramel lies in the fact you can anticipate the texture of each mouthful – real nursery food.

Butter 6 fairly shallow ramekins or small ovenproof dishes. Put the milk into a saucepan and add the mandarin zest and anise seeds, if using. Bring almost to the boil, then remove from the heat and leave to infuse.

Next make the caramel. Evenly sprinkle the sugar in a saucepan and pour in enough water to just cover the sugar. Heat on a medium heat until the sugar has melted and turned a rich amber colour. You can swirl the pan every so often, but resist stirring. Remove from the heat, then divide the caramel between the ramekins, working quickly.

Preheat the oven to 150°C/300°F/Gas mark 2. Whisk the whole eggs and egg yolks together with the sugar, just to combine. Don't let them become foamy and mousse-like. Strain the milk and gradually incorporate it into the egg and sugar mixture – again, don't whisk, just stir. Leave to stand while the caramel sets. If, after 15–20 minutes, the top is still a bit on the bubbly side, lightly skim it.

Pour the custard over the caramel, then cover each ramekin with foil. Put into a large roasting tin and pour in just-boiled water – it should come up to two-thirds of the way up the sides of the ramekins.

Cook the crème caramels in the oven for 15 minutes, then remove the foil and cook for a further 15 minutes, or until the custard still has a slight wobble in the middle. Remove the ramekins from the roasting tin and leave to cool completely, then cover and leave to chill in the refrigerator.

To serve, run a palette knife around the inside of each ramekin and upturn onto serving plates. The caramel should spill over the sides and pool around the set custard.

Honeycomb Jelly with Summer Fruits

Serves 6

Oil or cooking spray, for greasing
(optional; if turning out the jelly only)

Finely grated zest and juice of 2 large
lemons

3 eggs, separated

15g/½oz powdered gelatine

100g/½ cup caster (superfine) sugar

120ml/½ cup double (heavy) cream

400ml/1½ cups plus 2 tbsp milk

To serve

Fruit (I like strawberries or raspberries
in summer)

Double (heavy) cream (pouring
consistency)

1–2 tbsp limoncello (see page 248 for
homemade), to taste (optional)

**This is a childhood favourite. If I want to go all-out
retro, I will make it purely with lemon, but it can be
given more of a modern feel if you combine lemon
with bergamot, or yuzu and mandarin. You can make
individual versions of this – it will separate very prettily
in glass jars, but I love making it in a ring, filling the
centre with fruit and then flooding the whole thing with
pouring cream. The cream is all the better if it has had
a tablespoon or two of limoncello stirred through it.**

If you plan to turn out your jelly, lightly oil your mould or
glasses or spray with cooking spray.

Put the lemon zest, egg yolks, gelatine, sugar and cream
into a bowl and whisk until pale and thick. At the same
time, heat the milk in a saucepan until almost, but not
quite, boiling, remove from the heat and pour over the
egg yolk mixture, stirring as you go. It will help you
enormously if you put your bowl on a folded tea towel to
keep it steady while you do this.

Rinse out the milk pan and pour the mixture into it. Cook
on a very low heat, stirring constantly, until the mixture
has started to thicken. This will take anything between 5
and 10 minutes and is ready when it is the consistency
of crème anglaise. You should also be able to draw a line
through it when it coats the back of your wooden spoon.
Remove from the heat and allow to cool a little, then stir
in the lemon juice.

Whisk the egg whites in a bowl until they form stiff peaks.
Pour the custard into the egg whites, folding gently but
thoroughly until everything is well combined but you
haven't knocked too much air out of it.

Pour the mixture into your mould or into 6 individual
glasses. Put into the refrigerator to set – it will take at least
3 hours. When you are ready to serve, if turning out, dip
into a bowl of hot water for a few seconds, then turn out
onto a plate. Fill the centre with fruit if you like and serve
with thick cream, spiked or not with the limoncello.

Lychee and Mango Salad, with Yuzu, Mandarin and Black Pepper Syrup

Serves 4

2 mangoes, peeled and cut into strips

150g/5¼oz lychees, peeled, stoned and halved

A few basil leaves, torn, to garnish

Cracked black pepper

For the syrup

50g/3 tbsp runny honey

Finely grated zest and juice of 2 mandarins

2 tbsp yuzu juice

1 tsp powdered yuzu zest

½ tsp black peppercorns

For the cream

2 tsp runny honey

1 tsp grated fresh root ginger

200ml/generous ¾ cup crème fraîche

In this instance, if you can't find yuzu juice or zest, use lime instead.

Put the mango and lychees in a bowl. For the syrup, put the honey, mandarin zest and juice, yuzu juice, powdered zest and peppercorns into a small saucepan. Heat through gently until the honey has melted. Pour the whole lot over the mango and lychees. Allow to cool, then chill and leave to marinate until you are ready to serve.

When you are ready to serve, beat the honey and ginger into the crème fraîche. Pick the peppercorns out of the marinade. Serve the salad sprinkled with a few torn basil leaves, a crack of black pepper and the ginger cream on the side.

Orange and Fig Salad with Orange Blossom Ricotta and Pistachio Praline

Serves 4–6

8–12 figs, halved

3 tbsp runny honey

A pinch of ground cinnamon

A pinch of freshly ground black pepper

2 oranges, segmented (see page 15),
  peel and membranes reserved

200g/scant 1 cup ricotta

A few drops of orange blossom water

Fresh mint leaves, to garnish

For the praline

75g/6 tbsp granulated sugar

25ml/1 tbsp plus 2 tsp water

25g/⅕ cup shelled pistachios,
  roughly chopped

A large pinch of salt

It is usual to leave the figs whole, just cut down almost to the base, but I like them cut completely in half here as it makes for an easier assemblage on the plate.

You can double the amount of praline if you like as it's lovely to snack on. Alternatively, you can miss it out altogether and just lightly toast some pistachios or perhaps some hazelnuts instead.

First make the praline. Line a baking tray with baking parchment. Put the sugar and water in a small saucepan. Simmer on a low heat, stirring carefully until the sugar has dissolved, then turn up the heat and allow the syrup to bubble until it is a light golden brown – at this point it will be on the verge of turning a deeper colour and will be in danger of burning. Remove from the heat immediately and stir in the pistachios and salt. Tip out onto the baking tray and spread it out as much as possible. Leave to cool, by which point it will be hard and brittle. Blitz in a food processor to a powder.

Preheat the oven to 180°C/350°F/Gas mark 4. Put the figs cut side up in an ovenproof dish. Drizzle over 2 tablespoons of the honey and sprinkle with the cinnamon and black pepper. Roast for around 20 minutes. Remove from the oven and allow to cool a little. Arrange over a large serving bowl, plate, or individual serving bowls, with the orange segments.

Break up the ricotta in a bowl, using a fork. Add the remaining honey and the orange blossom water, then squeeze over the reserved orange peel and membranes to extract their juice. Whisk together into a cream. Spoon alongside the salad, sprinkle with the blitzed praline and serve topped with mint leaves.

Blood Orange and Rosemary Jelly

Serves 6

50g/¼ cup caster (superfine) sugar

3 small sprigs of rosemary, slightly bruised

50ml/3½ tbsp filtered, just-boiled water

350ml/1½ cups blood orange juice

Juice of ½ lemon

5 leaves of gelatine

Oil, for greasing

Quite a grown-up one this, and it can be made even more so if you use pink grapefruit juice in place of blood orange, as it, too, has an affinity with rosemary's piney notes.

I specify filtered water in this recipe purely because my own (London) water tends to be cloudy with lime and this does affect the clarity of the finished jelly.

Put the sugar in a bowl with the rosemary and pour over the just-boiled water. Stir until the sugar has dissolved – this gives an instant simple sugar syrup. Leave to infuse until cool.

If freshly squeezed, strain the blood orange and lemon juices into a measuring jug. Add the sugar syrup (including the rosemary) and some more filtered water until you have 500ml/2 cups plus 1 tbsp liquid.

Put the gelatine leaves in a heatproof bowl, then pour over some of the liquid. Leave to soften for around 10 minutes. Meanwhile, bring a saucepan of water to the boil. Set the bowl containing the gelatine over the pan and stir until it has melted. Pour in the rest of the liquid, then strain through a fine sieve into a clean jug.

Lightly oil a jelly mould or 6 individual moulds or glasses and pour in the strained liquid. When it has completely cooled down, refrigerate until set – it will take at least a couple of hours. To unmould, dip in hot water for a few seconds.

Earl Grey and Rose Parfait

Serves 8

3 tbsp Earl Grey tea leaves

150ml/10 tbsp water

100g/½ cup granulated sugar

4 egg yolks

300ml/1¼ cups whipping (heavy)
cream

1 tbsp vodka

A few drops of rose water, to taste

Oil, for greasing

The flavour of the bergamot really sings in a good-quality Earl Grey. This method takes time, because of the infusion, but cold infusing like this keeps the beautifully fresh flavour of the Earl Grey without waking up any of the bitter tannins (see more about this on page 237).

Put the tea leaves in a small glass jar or bottle and add the water. Cover and leave in the refrigerator to infuse for 24 hours.

Strain the infused water into a saucepan, add the sugar and heat gently until it has dissolved. Remove from the heat immediately and let it cool to blood temperature (it should feel comfortably warm, not too hot, when you dip your finger in).

Put the egg yolks in a large, heatproof bowl and, using an electric whisk, whisk until very frothy. Dribble the sugar syrup in a little at a time, whisking gently as you do so, until it is all incorporated. Continue to whisk the mixture until it has increased in volume considerably – at least doubled, preferably more. This will take up to 10 minutes.

Whisk the cream in a separate bowl until it is well aerated but still a soft dropping consistency. Fold it in into the egg and sugar mixture, very gently, preferably in 3–4 stages, being careful not to knock too much air out of it. Pour in the vodka and rose water at the last minute and stir again to incorporate.

Oil a large terrine or loaf tin (or individual moulds if you prefer; I have some owl-shaped ones I love) and line with plastic wrap, then pour in the parfait mixture. Freeze for at least 2–3 hours. When you are close to wanting to serve it, remove from the freezer and transfer to the refrigerator for 15–20 minutes, just to soften slightly. If turning it out whole, dip a knife in hot water to cut it.

Lime, Kaffir Lime and Basil Ice Cream

Makes about 1 litre/2 pints

Finely grated zest and juice of 3 limes (about 90ml/6 tbsp)

A few kaffir lime leaves, shredded

A large handful of basil sprigs

200g/2 cups caster (superfine) sugar

500ml/2 cups double (heavy) cream, well chilled

I bought a small kaffir lime tree several years ago, as I realized that it was much more cost-effective than paying exorbitant prices for small amounts of kaffir leaves. The leaves are fresher too. I don't usually like kaffir lime in sweet dishes – this is the one exception and came about when my tree (much larger now!) shed a large enough number of leaves to justify experimentation.

This is a simple way of getting a very fresh and intense flavour into ice cream as it is no-cook.

Put the lime zest and half the juice in a food processor and add the lime leaves, basil leaves and stalks, and the sugar.

Blitz until the mixture is green-flecked, then leave to stand for around an hour to give the flavours a chance to infuse – the sugar will dissolve during this time.

Strain the mixture then mix with the cream and the remaining lime juice. Churn in an ice-cream maker, then freeze. Remove from the freezer around 10 minutes before you want to serve it, to allow it to soften slightly.

Gin and Bitter Grapefruit Granita

Makes about 750ml/1½ pints

Finely grated zest and juice of 1
   grapefruit (yellow or pink)

A few sprigs of mint (grapefruit mint
   if you have it, spearmint otherwise)

125g/scant ⅔ cup granulated sugar

250ml/generous 1 cup water

250ml/generous 1 cup tonic water

50ml/3½ tbsp gin

Grapefruit bitters, to serve (optional)

**One of the best things about making my own cordials
has been matching them to favourite tipples.
I discovered both cordials on page 243 are wonderful
added to a gin and tonic, and this recipe takes similar
flavours to make a superbly refreshing granita. If you
happen to have made the grapefruit cordial, you could
add a slug of it too.**

Put the grapefruit zest, mint and sugar into a saucepan
with the water. Stir over a gentle heat until the sugar has
dissolved then turn up the heat and bring to the boil.
Remove from the heat immediately, then add the tonic
water, gin and grapefruit juice. Leave to cool to room
temperature, then chill in the refrigerator.

Strain the liquid into a lidded freezer-proof box. You need
it to be fairly wide, so the granita is quite shallow, about
2–3cm/1-in deep. Freeze for an hour, or until a layer of ice
has formed around the edge of the granita. Scrape this off
with a fork and beat into the rest of the mixture. Repeat
this every 30 minutes, until you have a granita formed of
ice crystals. Leave in the freezer until you are ready to eat,
but if you are leaving it for any length of time, you are
going to need to break it up fairly regularly. Serve in small
glasses, with a dash of grapefruit bitters, if you like.

Lemon Ice Cream with Almond and Fennel Praline

Makes about 800ml/1¾ pints

For the ice cream
Finely grated zest and juice of 3 lemons
150g/¾ cup granulated sugar
A pinch of salt
500ml/2 cups double (heavy) cream

For the almond and fennel seed praline
75g/½ cup blanched almonds, roughly chopped (you can also use flaked almonds)
1 tsp fennel seeds
A generous pinch of sea salt
150g/¾ cup granulated sugar
50ml/3½ tbsp water

This is the best method for a no-cook ice cream I've found, based loosely on one in the manual from my 20-year-old ice-cream maker. It is beautifully fresh tasting – sherbety, even – and much nicer than lemon sorbet.

I have also made this ice cream using a combination of lemon and orange, with a praline of pistachios and cardamom seeds. Well worth trying.

Put the lemon zest in a food processor with the sugar and salt. Blitz until the zest has all but vanished into the sugar – this will ensure you get a perfectly smooth ice cream.

Add the juice from 2 of the lemons and blitz again, this time to dissolve the sugar. Pour this mixture into the cream and combine thoroughly. Leave to chill in the refrigerator for at least an hour.

To make the praline, line a baking tray with baking parchment. Mix the almonds, fennel seeds and salt together. Put the sugar and water in a small saucepan. Simmer on a low heat, stirring carefully until the sugar has dissolved, then turn up the heat and allow the syrup to bubble until it is a light golden brown – at this point it will be on the verge of turning a deeper colour and will be in danger of burning. Remove from the heat immediately and stir in the almond mixture. Tip out onto the lined baking tray and spread it out as much as possible. Leave to cool, by which point it will be hard and brittle. Break into chunks.

Taste the chilled cream mixture and add a little more lemon juice if you think it needs it. Churn in an ice-cream maker until thick, smooth and aerated. Stir around half the praline (save the rest for another occasion) through the ice cream at this point, and churn for a further minute. Scrape into a freezer container and freeze. Remove from the freezer 10 minutes before you want to serve it.

3 Classic Ice Lollies

I was one of those children who, when offered an ice lolly, would always want a classic lemon ice in favour of something more complicated (or lurid, depending on your point of view). The recipes here very much take inspiration from those, with options for adding alcohol if they are strictly adult-only.

Makes about 8

15g/2½ tbsp loose black tea (a good English breakfast is fine)

Pared zest and juice of ½ lemon

500ml/2 cups plus 1 tbsp water, preferably filtered

50g/¼ cup granulated sugar

8 thin slices of lemon (optional)

Lemon Iced Tea Ice Lolly

This is a very simple one, and is based on the cold-brewed teas you will find on page 237. This means you can easily vary the flavours – just substitute whatever type of tea or citrus you fancy.

If you want to make these very pretty, you can add a slice of lemon to each so it appears, ghostlike, through the ice.

Put the tea in a refrigerator-friendly receptacle with the pared zest and pour over the water. Refrigerate overnight to brew. You will find it tastes fairly strong without any of the bitter tannins.

The next day, strain the tea and discard the solids. Add the lemon juice and sugar, stir until it has completely dissolved, then taste. It may need a squeeze more lemon or more sugar – just remember that the sweetness will be weaker once frozen, so don't make it too sour.

Pour the liquid into your lolly moulds. If you have the sort with the plastic reuseable tops put these in straight away. Otherwise wait until the ice lolly has set hard enough to hold a wooden ice lolly stick, then put one in each. This is also the point where you would add a lemon slice, if using, but obviously do this first. Freeze until firm – as this is a water-based lolly it should be frozen within 3–4 hours.

Makes about 8

A small bunch of mint, leaves only

Pared zest of 1 lime and 75ml/5 tbsp lime juice

250ml/1 cup plus 1 tbsp double (heavy) cream or coconut milk

250g/8¾oz melon, prepared weight

100g/½ cup granulated sugar

Lime, Melon and Mint Ice Lolly

Use a green-fleshed melon for this if you can, to help preserve the green colour. This is one that you can happily add alcohol to – try a couple of tablespoons of rum or tequila – or have a little bowl of it to hand for dipping when you eat it.

Put the mint leaves and lime zest in a bowl and muddle them as much as possible to bruise the mint and release oils from the zest. Put the cream or coconut milk in a small saucepan and heat gently until almost boiling. Remove from the heat and add the mint leaves and lime zest. Leave to infuse for as long as you can – at least until the liquid is completely cool – then strain into a blender. Add the melon, lime juice and sugar and blitz until smooth, then push through a sieve into a clean jug.

Pour into your ice lolly moulds (see page 184) and freeze until solid.

Makes about 8

100g/½ cup caster (superfine) sugar

50ml/3½ tbsp water

Pared zest of 2 mandarins and 500ml/ generous 2 cups mandarin juice (from around 12 mandarins)

50ml/3½ tbsp yuzu juice

1 tsp powdered yuzu zest (optional)

Mandarin and Yuzu Ice Lolly

This is a very refreshing, sharp-tasting ice lolly. If you like, you can add a measure of vodka or sake to the mixture, taking out the same amount of mandarin juice – or dip the lollies in either one as you eat them, as above.

Put the sugar in a small pan with the water and mandarin zest. Stir over a low heat until the sugar has dissolved. Remove from the heat and leave to cool to room temperature.

Strain the sugar syrup, then stir in the mandarin and yuzu juices, and the powdered yuzu zest, if using. Pour into your ice lolly moulds (see page 184) and freeze until solid.

Lime, Cinnamon and Rum Sorbet

Makes about 1 litre/2 pints

300g/1½ cups soft light brown sugar

300ml/1¼ cups water

1 large cinnamon stick

Pared zest and juice of 3 limes

125ml/½ cup plus 1 tsp golden rum

250ml/1 cup plus 1 tbsp good quality lemon or limeade, or tonic water

To serve

Angostura bitters

Freshly grated nutmeg

This sorbet is based on a punch recipe I love, from Dominica – it makes a wonderful sorbet, but I prefer to blitz the frozen sorbet and serve as a kind of slush. The type of soft drink you use here really does impact on the taste of the sorbet. I like organic lemonade, but have also been known to use Ting, a sparkling grapefruit drink from the Caribbean.

Put the sugar, water and cinnamon stick in a saucepan. Simmer over a low heat, stirring constantly, until the sugar has dissolved, then continue to simmer very gently for 10 minutes. Add the lime zest and simmer for a further 5 minutes, then leave to cool.

Strain the syrup into a bowl, then mix with the lime juice, rum and your soft drink of choice. Churn in an ice-cream maker for around 30 minutes (it won't thicken properly at this stage, because of the alcohol – the upside to this being that it will freeze to a state that is scoopable as soon as you remove it from the freezer).

Serve in scoops (or blitz to a slush, see introduction) with a dash of bitters and a rasp of nutmeg.

A Very Adaptable Citrus Sorbet

Makes about 750ml/1½ pints

100g/½ cup granulated sugar

400ml/1½ cups plus 2 tbsp water

Finely grated zest of 1 citrus fruit
 (½ if grapefruit)

125ml/½ cup plus 1 tsp sour
 citrus juice

Citrus sorbets, especially lemon or lime, are always popular – use this method to apply to any of the sourer fruits, including grapefruit and bitter oranges. If you decide on bergamot, it is well to do half bergamot, half lemon or lime, as it can be particularly sour, or instead use some Earl Grey tea in the infusion. I also really love combining mandarin, lemon and yuzu together.

I find it almost impossible to make these unadulterated – a good glug of liqueur or "cello" is great at the end and helps make a softer sorbet. Otherwise you can serve them with a shot of spirit or liqueur poured over. Try lemon with a shot of gin, lime with white rum or tequila, a combination of mandarin and yuzu with vodka or sake. In terms of other flavour notes, you can also add other aromatics – I love cinnamon with lime, star anise with grapefruit, bay leaves with lemon, Szechuan peppercorns with orange.

Put the sugar and water into a saucepan and add the citrus zest. Stir over a low heat until the sugar is dissolved. Remove from the heat, cool to room temperature, then chill in the refrigerator for at least 1 hour. Stir in the citrus juice, then strain. Churn in an ice-cream maker until thick and well aerated, then transfer to a freezer container and freeze.

Serve as it is or with a good glug of a favourite liqueur poured over.

Grapefruit, Honey and Cinnamon Fool with Cinnamon Snaps

Serves 6

50g/3 tbsp runny honey (I like a very floral orange blossom)

75ml/5 tbsp sweet wine (I use Moscatel)

Finely grated zest and juice of ½ grapefruit

A pinch of ground cinnamon

A dash of bitters (optional)

300ml/1¼ cups whipping (heavy) cream.

This is the simplest of desserts – probably the quickest in this chapter – but it has a surprisingly complex flavour, especially if you use Moscatel, which gives wonderfully nutty undertones.

You can serve any biscuit or cookie with this but I do like these cinnamon rum snaps. You could even whisk the cream until slightly thicker and pipe the fool into the snaps if you prefer.

Mix together the honey, sweet wine, grapefruit zest and juice and the cinnamon – you should find it will end up the texture of a thinnish syrup. Add a dash of bitters if you like. Start whisking the cream until increasing in volume and becoming soft and billowy. Pour in the honey and grapefruit mixture and continue whisking for as short a time as possible – you don't want this remotely stiff. Add a little more grapefruit juice if it firms up too much. Pour into individual glasses.

50g/3½ tbsp butter, plus extra for greasing

50g/¼ cup soft light brown sugar

50g/3 tbsp runny honey

1 tbsp rum

A dash of bitters (optional)

50g/6 tbsp plain (all-purpose) flour

½ tsp ground cinnamon

A pinch of salt

Cinnamon Rum Snaps

Preheat the oven to 180°C/350°F/Gas mark 4. Butter 2 large baking trays.

Put the butter, sugar and honey into a small saucepan and heat gently until everything has melted together. Remove from the heat and stir in the rum and the bitters, if using. Sprinkle over the flour and cinnamon with the salt, then beat everything to combine.

Drop heaped teaspoons of the mixture onto the baking trays, spacing them out well. Cook one tray at a time, for 7–8 minutes. When the snaps have spread across the trays and are just very lightly coloured, remove from the oven.

Leave for a minute or two – the biscuits should be hard enough not to collapse, but soft enough to manipulate. Wrap each biscuit around a slim handle, making sure the edges overlap. Remove and leave to cool, then repeat with the second tray.

Baking

Something transformative happens when you combine citrus with butter, sugar and eggs – and, unusually, here I mean the citrus is transformed – captured and enhanced by those ingredients, rather than the other way round. This is especially true of lemons and oranges, but try any of the cake recipes in this chapter with grapefruit and you will be amazed at how complex and rounded the flavour becomes.

As usual, all of these are adaptable. The Classic Drizzle Cake (page 192), in particular, *sans* syrup, is very similar to a Madeira cake and is happy with any citrus flavour you care to throw at it. It is probably the cake I make most frequently.

There is a cake for virtually every mood and season here, including Christmas, although I haven't followed the traditional route of a dark fruit cake, rich with candied peel and zest. I think there is enough richness to Christmas, what with the pudding and mincemeat, so instead I have made a lighter Bundt cake that is almost a cross between a Christmas cake and a panettone (page 211). If you want something dark, try the Rum and Marmalade Loaf Cake (page 204), which is an excellent keeping cake and wonderful spread with butter.

Citrus Butter Biscuits

Makes about 48

200g/¾ cup plus 2 tbsp butter, softened

200g/1 cup golden caster (superfine) sugar, plus extra for sprinkling

Finely grated zest of 2 small or 1 large citrus

2 eggs

500g/3¾ cups plain (all-purpose) flour

Candied Citrus Zest (see page 216), finely chopped (optional)

I love these. No rolling out, no piping, just cut-and-come-again from the refrigerator, or freezer. It means you can bake as many or as few as you like at a time. My favourite flavour for these is mandarin, but you can use any citrus or a combination.

Put the butter into the bowl of a stand mixer (or a large bowl if using an electric hand whisk). Add the sugar, then beat until the mixture is very soft, fluffy and white. Add the grated zest and beat for another minute.

Add the eggs, one at a time, with 2 tablespoons of flour in between each addition, to stop the mixture from curdling, then incorporate the rest of the flour. Do not over-work as you don't want the mixture to be too tough. If using the candied citrus zest, add it at this point too.

Roll the mixture into 4 fat logs – at least 5–6cm/2–2½-in diameter. Wrap and chill in the refrigerator until you want to bake them, but for at least 2 hours.

When you are ready to cook the biscuits, preheat the oven to 180°C/350°F/Gas mark 4. Cut the biscuits in 0.5cm/¼-in slices; you should get about 12 slices from each log. Space evenly on a large baking tray then bake for 10–12 minutes, until a very light golden brown. Remove and transfer immediately to a cooling rack, and sprinkle with sugar.

Note

If you want to freeze the uncooked logs, it is better to chill them well and cut into slices first. Open freeze until hard then transfer to a bag. You can cook them from frozen – they will take between 18 and 20 minutes.

Classic Drizzle Cake

Serves 10–12

250g/1 cup plus 2 tbsp unsalted butter, softened, plus extra for greasing

200g/1 cup caster (superfine) sugar

Finely grated zest and juice of 2 mandarins

Finely grated zest of 1 lime

3 large eggs

300g/2¼ cups self-raising (self-rising) flour

For the syrup

Finely grated zest and juice of 2 limes

Finely grated zest and juice of 2 mandarins

150g/about 1 cup icing (confectioners') sugar

1 tbsp tequila (optional)

This is probably the cake I make more than any other, but it is rarely the same twice. The basic recipe is very reliable and lends itself to all kinds of flavour variations. The traditionally subtle addition of lemon is wonderful, but this is my absolute favourite – mandarin and lime, with a tequila-spiked syrup.

Preheat the oven to 170°C/340°F/Gas mark 3½. Butter a large (900g/2lb) loaf tin and line it with baking parchment.

Cream the butter, sugar and citrus zests together until very pale, fluffy and increased in volume. Add the eggs one at a time, along with 2 tablespoons of the flour, then incorporate the remaining flour. Using a light hand, mix in the mandarin juice – you should have a batter with a reluctant dropping consistency.

Scrape into the loaf tin, then bake in the oven for approximately 1 hour – it is done when it has slightly shrunk away from the sides and a skewer comes out clean.

While the cake is baking, make the syrup. Put the zests, juices and sugar into a saucepan and warm through gently on a low heat until the sugar has dissolved. Stir in the tequila, if using.

Pierce the cake all over with a cocktail stick or similar, then pour over the syrup, trying to make sure most of it goes into the centre of the cake, rather than around the edges. Leave the cake to cool in the tin until it is completely cold.

Liquorice and Lemon Sherbet Fairy Cakes

Makes 12

50ml/3½ tbsp milk

50g/1¾oz soft liquorice

100g/7 tbsp butter, softened

100g/½ cup golden caster (superfine) sugar

100g/¾ cup plain (all-purpose) flour

½ tsp baking powder

2 eggs

For the icing

10g/⅓oz Candied Citrus Zest (see page 216), plus extra for decoration

200g/1½ cups icing (confectioners') sugar

My adoration of the liquorice/sherbet combination has lasted well into adulthood – I have even been presented with whole boxes of Sherbet Fountains by people-in-the-know. If you want a sherbety flavour here but aren't keen on the liquorice, you can make a regular fairy (cup) cake, replacing the milk and liquorice with the grated zest and juice of 1 lemon and enough milk to make a dropping consistency.

Preheat the oven to 180°C/350°F/Gas mark 4. Line a fairy (cup) cake tin with paper cases.

Put the milk and liquorice in a small saucepan and heat very gently until the liquorice has almost completely melted. Remove from the heat and leave to cool to blood temperature.

Cream the butter and sugar together in a large bowl until very light and fluffy. Whisk the flour and baking powder together just to combine and get rid of any lumps. Add the eggs to the beaten butter and sugar one at a time, adding a tablespoon of flour between each, then fold in the rest of the flour. Pour in the milk and liquorice mixture and stir until combined, then add a little more milk if the batter isn't at proper dropping consistency.

Spoon the mixture into the paper cases – they should only be around half full. Bake for around 15–20 minutes, then remove from the oven and cool completely.

To make the icing, blitz the candied zest with the icing (confectioners') sugar in a small food processor until powdery. Reserve a couple of tablespoons of this mixture for sprinkling, then add boiling water to the remainder, a teaspoon at a time, until you have a thick, spoonable glacé icing – do not let it get too runny. Spoon the icing onto the cakes. When it has set, sprinkle with the reserved sugar and decorate with more candied citrus zest.

Madeleines

Makes 24 small or 12 large

100g/7 tbsp butter, plus extra for greasing

100g/½ cup caster (superfine) sugar

2 eggs

100g/¾ cup plain (all-purpose) flour, plus extra for dusting

½ tsp baking powder

Finely grated zest and juice of 1 lemon

A proper madeleine – buttery, airy and lightly fragrant – is one of those things that I feel should not be messed around with. I see recipes adding nuts or honey, dousing them in syrup or coating them with chocolate, or – horror of horrors! – jam and desiccated coconut. This is wrong. I'm afraid I am prepared to do nothing more to them than vary the type of citrus I use – and I may be tempted to add a few drops of orange blossom water if making them with anything other than lemon. If eaten within the hour, as recommended, they do not need anything else.

Gently melt the butter, then set aside and allow to cool to blood temperature. Whisk the sugar and eggs together in a bowl until well combined and slightly frothy and aerated. Whisk in the remaining ingredients, including the melted butter. Cover and chill in the refrigerator for at least 1 hour, or several if possible – this will help form the traditional "bump" that is so distinctively "madeleine".

When you are almost ready to bake the madeleines, preheat the oven to 180°C/350°F/Gas mark 4. Melt a little more butter and use it to brush two madeleine tins (or one; you can bake these in two batches), then dust with flour and turn upside down and drop onto a surface to remove the excess. Spoon in the madeleine batter – a dessertspoon for each should do it, but make sure you don't over-fill the mould; they should only be around two-thirds full. Bake in the oven for 8–10 minutes until golden brown, slightly darker around the edges and shrunken away slightly from the tin.

Turn out onto a wire rack to cool and try to eat within the hour.

Orange and Ginger Butter Shortbread

Makes 8 slices

150g/¾ cup golden caster (superfine) sugar

250g/1¾ cups plus 2 tbsp plain (all-purpose) flour

75g/2½oz ground almonds

A pinch of salt

Finely grated zest of 1 orange or grapefruit

200g/¾ cup plus 2 tbsp butter, softened

1 egg yolk, plus 1 whole egg, beaten, to glaze

50g/2½ tbsp stem ginger

50g/2½ tbsp finely chopped candied citrus peel (orange or grapefruit; see page 218 for homemade)

50g/2½ tbsp pine nuts

Icing (confectioners') sugar, for dusting

This is a lovely buttery shortbread, studded with stem ginger and candied peel – I use orange or grapefruit here, but you can use any you prefer; lemon is good too. It is based on the Dutch shortbread Boterkoek, which I first came across in Gaitri Pagrach-Chandra's wonderful *Warm Bread and Honey Cake*.

Put the sugar, flour and ground almonds in a large bowl and add the salt. Whisk to combine and remove any lumps. Add the zest, butter, egg yolk, stem ginger, citrus peel and pine nuts, and lightly knead everything together until you have a dough.

Shape the dough into a fairly flat round, then either lightly roll out or press into a 24cm/9½-in round tin. Chill well in the refrigerator, preferably overnight, then bring back to room temperature. Preheat the oven to 180°C/350°F/Gas mark 4.

Score lines in the dough to mark out 8 portions. Brush with the beaten egg and bake in the oven for 25–30 minutes. The dough should colour only very lightly, if at all, and should still be soft when it comes out of the oven. Leave to cool, then dust with icing (confectioners') sugar and cut into slices, following the score lines you marked before baking. Store in an airtight tin.

Variation

The ginger version packs a punch, but for something sweeter and more mellow, just omit the ginger and add around a teaspoon of orange blossom water with the egg. Keep the candied peel and pine nuts!

Lemon Curd Slices

Makes 12–18

For the shortbread

250g/1¾ cups plus 2 tbsp plain (all-purpose) flour

75g/8½ tbsp icing (confectioners') sugar

A pinch of salt

200g/¾ cup plus 2 tbsp butter, chilled and diced

2 tbsp milk

1 egg yolk

1 quantity Lemon Curd (see page 224)

For the crumble topping

100g/¾ cup plain (all-purpose) flour (or 50/50 flour and ground almonds)

25g/2 tbsp caster (superfine) sugar

A pinch of salt

50g/3½ tbsp butter

1 egg yolk

These hark back to my school days. More or less every day we had a variation on a pastry- or shortbread-based slice – bananas with jam and custard, gypsy tart, the hated cornflakes one – and then these. I make these to go in the children's lunchboxes as a special treat. You can use any kind of curd here as well as adding different spices to the crumble mix – I love ground ginger with lime curd.

For the shortbread, put the flour, icing (confectioners') sugar and salt in a bowl or food processor and either rub in or process with the butter until resembling breadcrumbs. Add the milk and egg yolk and bring the dough together into a ball. Flatten out a little, then wrap in plastic wrap and chill in the refrigerator for at least 30 minutes.

Roll out the chilled dough and use it to line a 30 x 20cm/11¾ x 8-in Swiss roll or brownie tin. Chill for a further 15 minutes. Preheat the oven to 180°C/350°F/ Gas mark 4.

Prod the shortbread all over with a fork then bake for around 20 minutes until lightly golden.

For the crumble topping, mix the flour, sugar and salt together, then rub in the butter. Lightly mix in the egg yolk – this will allow the mixture to clump together a little, which is exactly what you need here. Remove the shortbread from the oven and spread the lemon curd over as evenly as you can. Sprinkle the topping over the lemon curd.

Return to the oven to bake for a further 20 minutes until the crumble topping is golden brown. Cool slightly before you cut into slices.

Lime, Chamomile and Honey Cake

Serves 8–10

250g/1 cup plus 2 tbsp butter, softened, plus extra for greasing

2 tbsp dried chamomile (or equivalent in tea bags)

50ml/3½ tbsp boiling water

175g/¾ cup plus 2 tbsp golden caster (superfine) sugar

Finely grated zest of 2 limes

75g/4 tbsp runny honey

300g/2¼ cups plain (all-purpose) flour

2 tsp baking powder

3 eggs

For the filling

200ml/generous ¾ cup double (heavy) cream

1 tbsp runny honey

Finely grated zest of 1 lime

Fruit, such as blackberries, raspberries or strawberries (optional)

To decorate

Icing (confectioners') sugar

Fresh or dried chamomile flowers

Variation

This is also very good using elderflower in place of the chamomile, in which case you can use either lime or lemon zest. Add a squeeze of citrus juice to the cake batter too.

I find this quite a soothing cake to eat, accompanied by some plain white tea. Its flavour will vary depending on the type of honey you use – to complement the lime and chamomile I normally choose lime or orange blossom. It will also work well with a layer of fruit in the middle with the cream. Try blackberries, raspberries or strawberries.

Preheat the oven to 180°C/350°F/Gas mark 4. Butter and line 2 x 20cm/8-in Victoria sandwich tins.

Place 1 tablespoon of the chamomile in a bowl and pour the boiling water over. Leave to steep until cooled. Blitz the remaining chamomile with the sugar and lime zest.

Beat the butter, blitzed sugar and honey together until aerated and fluffy. Whisk the flour and baking powder together in a separate bowl. Gradually incorporate the eggs into the beaten butter and sugar, alternating with tablespoons of flour, then gently fold in the remaining flour. Strain the steeped chamomile and add enough of the liquid to the cake batter to give a dropping consistency.

Divide the batter between the prepared tins. Bake in the oven for around 20–25 minutes until the cakes are springy to touch, a light golden brown, and have started to shrink away from the sides. Leave to cool in the tins for a few minutes then turn out onto a wire rack to cool completely.

To make the filling, whisk the cream, honey and lime zest together until stiff enough to pile onto one of the cakes. Spread evenly onto a cooled cake, then add fruit, if you like. Top with the remaining cake, then dust with icing (confectioners') sugar and decorate with chamomile flowers.

Jaffa Cakes

Makes 24

For the base

A little softened butter or cooking
spray, for greasing

2 eggs

60g/5 tbsp caster (superfine) sugar

60g/7½ tbsp plain (all-purpose) flour

30g/2 tbsp butter, melted and cooled
to blood temperature

For the jelly centre

50ml/3½ tbsp lemon juice

Finely grated zest of 1 orange and
100ml/7 tbsp juice

Finely grated zest of 1 lime

25g/2 tbsp caster (superfine) sugar

3 gelatine leaves

For the chocolate topping

150g/5¼oz dark chocolate

Dried zest of ½ orange (see page 18),
finely ground

A little edible gold powder (optional)

**The cake base for this is almost identical to that of
madeleines (see page 195) – it's a slightly unusual
method, but makes for a cake that keeps its shape
and should provide a flat, even base for the jelly and
chocolate. I've used a mixture of orange, lemon and
lime here; I really like the combination.**

First make the jelly as this needs time to set thoroughly.
Put the lemon and orange juices into a small pan with
the orange and lime zests and the sugar and heat gently,
stirring, until the sugar has dissolved. Meanwhile, soak
the gelatine leaves in cold water until soft. Squeeze out
and add to the liquid, stirring until they have completely
dissolved. Line a small roasting tin with plastic wrap and
pour the liquid into it. Leave to cool to room temperature
then refrigerate for several hours until completely set.

To make the sponge base, preheat the oven to
180°C/350°F/Gas mark 4. Lightly butter 2 x 12-hole
muffin tins, or spray with cooking oil. Put the eggs and
sugar in a bowl and beat with an electric whisk for several
minutes until increased in volume, mousse-like and the
colour of pale apricot. Sift the flour into the mixture and
fold in, then add the melted butter. Spoon the mixture
into the muffin tins – each should take a tablespoon. Bake
in the oven for 8–10 minutes until lightly golden brown.

Leave to cool for a few minutes then remove from the tin
– they should just flip straight out, but if not, prise them
out gently with a palette knife. When they are completely
cool, cut the set jelly into 4cm/1½-in rounds (use a small
shot glass if you don't have a cutter that size) and place
on top, as centrally as you can. Melt the chocolate in a
bain marie or heatproof bowl set over a pan of simmering
water, then use it to completely coat the tops of the cakes.
You will find that you need a heaped teaspoon per cake.
Make sure that the chocolate isn't too hot when you start
or the jelly might melt or sweat a little. Leave the chocolate
to set somewhere cool before eating, then dust with
powdered orange zest, mixed with edible gold powder,
if you have some.

Mr Happy's Sunshine Cake

Serves 12–16

200g/¾ cup plus 2 tbsp butter, softened, plus extra for greasing

175g/¾ cup plus 2 tbsp golden caster (superfine) sugar

Finely grated zest of 2 lemons

300g/2 cups cornmeal or polenta (a fine, slightly sandy textured one)

2 tsp baking powder

3 eggs

For the syrup (optional)
Juice of 2 lemons

125g/¾ cup plus 2 tbsp icing (confectioners') sugar

Variations

I have made this with most citrus and find lemon works best, but grapefruit (using the juice of just 1 grapefruit) also works beautifully. I also like adding other flavours to the syrup. Try finely ground cardamom with the lemon, and rosemary with the grapefruit.

The combination of lemon and polenta here ensures that when you cut through the crust of the cake you find a mood-lifting, sunny interior, just the sort of thing to eat on a gloomy winter's day when you want to snuggle on the sofa with a cosy blanket and a big mug of tea.

This cake is usually made with a mixture of cornmeal and ground almonds, which is lovely – but I wanted to include at least one cake that is very economical, and this one is if you aren't forking out for almonds. If you do want to include almonds, substitute half the cornmeal. Oh, and the syrup is strictly optional.

Preheat the oven to 180°C/350°F/Gas mark 4. Grease and line a 23cm/9-in round, loose-bottomed cake tin.

Beat the butter, sugar and lemon zest together in a bowl, until the volume has dramatically increased and the texture is soft and airy.

Mix the cornmeal or polenta with the baking powder. Add the eggs to the creamed butter and sugar one at a time with a couple of tablespoons of the cornmeal, beating well between each addition, then add the rest of the cornmeal. The mixture will be fairly dry, certainly not as loose as a dropping consistency. Don't worry, this is as it should be.

Scrape the batter into the prepared cake tin and smooth over a little. Bake in the oven for around 35–40 minutes, until it is a deep golden brown and has shrunk away from the sides of the cake tin.

Meanwhile, make the syrup, if using. Put the lemon juice and icing (confectioners') sugar into a small saucepan and stir over a low heat until the sugar has dissolved and the texture is syrupy. While the cake is still hot, pierce the top all over with a cocktail stick or something similarly pointy. Pour the syrup over the cake as evenly as possible. Leave to cool completely before serving, with a dollop of crème fraîche, if you like.

Blood Orange, Pomegranate and Hazelnut Meringue Cake

Serves 10–12

For the meringue

A little softened butter, for greasing

4 egg whites

250g/1¼ cups caster (superfine) sugar

½ tsp white vinegar

½ tsp vanilla extract

125g/1 cup skinned hazelnuts, toasted and finely ground

For the filling

500ml/generous 2 cups double (heavy) cream

1 tbsp icing (confectioners') sugar

1 quantity blood orange or Seville orange curd (see page 224)

Seeds from 1 pomegranate

To decorate

Strips of pared blood orange zest or candied zest (see page 216)

Variation

This can be made with a chocolate ganache in place of the pomegranate seeds. Simply melt together equal quantities of chocolate and double (heavy) cream – around 100g/3½oz of each – and when it has cooled to a spreadable consistency, use a palette knife to spread over two of the meringue rounds before topping with the cream and curd.

This looks very pure and elegant, until it is cut into and then turns into a riot of colour. Despite the amount of cream, it is actually a remarkably light, refreshing cake to serve at the end of a meal.

Preheat the oven to 160°C/325°F/Gas mark 3. Butter and line 3 x 20cm/8-in sandwich tins.

To make the meringue, first weigh a large mixing bowl (to ensure an even split of mixture when dividing it between the tins). In the bowl, whisk the egg whites to the soft peak stage, then gradually whisk in the sugar. When the meringue is stiff and glossy, add the vinegar and vanilla and whisk again. Stir in the ground hazelnuts.

Weigh the mixture in the bowl and subtract the initial bowl weight from the total – it's then simple to divide by 3 and spoon an equal amount into each tin.

Smooth down the meringue with a palette knife, making it as even as possible. Bake in the oven for around 25 minutes, until lightly golden brown, then remove from the oven and leave to cool before removing from the tins.

Whisk the cream with the icing (confectioners') sugar until thick enough to spread.

To assemble, spread around 3–4 tablespoons of the cream on top of one of the meringue layers. Drizzle with a couple of tablespoons of curd (this is quite a runny curd) then sprinkle over half the pomegranate seeds. Top and repeat with the second layer, then top with the final meringue. Cover the whole cake – top and sides – with the remaining cream. Decorate with a few long strips of pared blood orange zest or even candied zest if you have any, or have the inclination to make some.

Rum and Marmalade Loaf Cake

Serves 10–12

175g/⅓ cup plus 1 tsp butter, softened, plus extra for greasing

100g/¾ cup raisins

100ml/7 tbsp rum

175g/1⅓ cups wholemeal (wholewheat) spelt flour

2 tsp baking powder

1 tsp ground ginger

1 tsp ground mixed spice

175g/¾ cup plus 2 tbsp dark muscovado sugar

Finely grated zest of 1 lime

150g/½ cup marmalade

3 eggs

To glaze

2 tbsp marmalade

1 tbsp rum (optional)

A good keeping cake this, if wrapped up well and left somewhere dark. I use the Dark and Stormy Marmalade on page 223 to make it, but you can use any other sort – just add 50g/⅓ cup finely chopped stem ginger to the cake as well, if you do.

Preheat the oven to 180°C/350°F/Gas mark 4. Butter and line a 1kg/2-lb loaf tin.

Put the raisins in a small saucepan and add the rum. Bring to the boil, then immediately remove from the heat and leave to stand while you make the rest of the cake.

Put the flour in a bowl with the baking powder and spices. Whisk together to combine and remove any lumps.

Beat the butter and sugar together in another bowl with the lime zest until very soft, and lightened to the colour of butterscotch. Beat in the marmalade, then add the eggs one at a time, adding a couple of tablespoons of the flour mixture with each addition. Stir through the rum-infused raisins along with any liquid that hasn't been absorbed.

Scrape the mixture into the prepared loaf tin and bake in the oven for around 1 hour, until well risen and a rich brown. For the glaze, melt the marmalade and rum, if using, together in a small saucepan and brush over the cake while it is still warm. Leave to cool in the tin. If you can bear to wrap this up and leave it for a couple of days, it will be all the better for it.

Orange and Pistachio Cake

Serves 12–16

2 oranges

Softened butter, for greasing

6 eggs

225g/1 cup plus 2 tbsp caster
(superfine) sugar

250g/1⅔ cups pistachios, finely ground

1 tsp baking powder

1 tbsp orange blossom water

To decorate

1 tbsp caster (superfine) sugar

50g/⅓ cup nibbed pistachios

A handful of dried rose petals

To serve

200ml/generous ¾ cup double
(heavy) cream

15g/1¾ tbsp icing (confectioners') sugar

1 tsp orange blossom water

The original orange and almond version of this cake is usually described as Sephardic; I first came across it via Claudia Roden and have been making variants on it for years. It does lend itself well to all kinds of citrus and nuts. I have tried clementines, blood oranges and a combination of oranges and limes, which have all been very good. This, however, is my favourite. It is extremely moist and has excellent keeping properties – in fact, it is usually better after a day or two.

Put the oranges in a saucepan and cover with just-boiled water. Return to the boil and simmer for a couple of hours, until tender – a good way to test this is to see how easily you can break the skin with the handle of a wooden spoon. Alternatively, you can pressure cook the oranges for 30 minutes. Drain the oranges and either run under cold water or wait for them to cool down naturally. As soon as they are cool enough to hold, break them open and remove any seeds. Blitz everything – white membrane, pith and all – in a food processor or blender, until smooth.

Preheat the oven to 190°C/375°F/Gas mark 5. Butter a 21–23cm/8½–9-in loose-bottomed cake tin and line the base with baking parchment.

Break the eggs into a bowl and whisk until frothy, then beat in the sugar, ground pistachios, baking powder and orange blossom water. Stir in the puréed oranges.

Pour the cake batter into the prepared tin. Bake in the oven for 1 hour–1 hour 20 minutes, depending on the size tin you use (a smaller size will make a deeper cake, which will need a little longer to cook). When the cake is done, a skewer will come out fairly clean.

Leave to cool in the tin for 15 minutes, then turn out onto a cooling rack. Dust with the caster (superfine) sugar and sprinkle with the nibbed pistachios and rose petals.

Whisk the cream with the icing (confectioners') sugar until it forms soft waves, then stir in the orange blossom water. Serve with slices of the cake.

Orange, Pecan and Cinnamon Rolls

Makes 12

For the dough

250ml/1 cup plus 1 tbsp milk

75g/⅓ cup butter

350g/2⅔ cups strong white bread flour

150g/1 cup plus 2 tbsp wholemeal (wholewheat) spelt flour

10g/⅓oz instant dried yeast

75g/⅓ cup soft light brown sugar

A large pinch of salt

1 egg

Finely grated zest of 1 orange

Oil, for greasing

For the filling

50g/⅓ cup raisins

50ml/3½ tbsp bourbon

100g/scant ½ cup butter, softened, plus extra for greasing

50ml/3½ tbsp maple syrup

25g/2 tbsp soft dark brown sugar

1 tsp ground cinnamon

1 tsp ground mixed spice

A pinch of salt

75g/¾ cup chopped pecans

50g/1¾oz finely chopped candied orange peel (see page 218 for homemade)

To glaze

1 egg, beaten

1 tbsp orange marmalade

1 tbsp soft light brown sugar

1 tbsp bourbon or water

These are extremely satisfying to make, and even more satisfying to pull apart and eat. I particularly love that the rolls can push themselves up when I have optimistically crammed them in a little too tightly – it means you get slightly more surface area to glaze and a little more caramelization.

Put the milk in a saucepan and bring up to almost boiling point. Remove from the heat and add the butter. Leave to stand until the butter has melted and it has cooled to blood temperature.

Put the flours in a large bowl with the yeast, sugar and salt. Make a well in the middle. Beat the egg into the milk and butter mixture and stir in the orange zest. Add this to the flour and stir until well combined – you will find that you have a very soft, sticky dough.

Lightly oil your hands and the work surface, then turn out the dough. Knead by sliding your fingers under the dough, pulling it up, and slapping it back down onto the work surface. When you move your hands up away from the dough it will come with you – stretch it upwards and to the sides at the same time, then tuck it back under when you repeat the whole motion of lifting it again. After a few minutes you will have a dough that is no longer sticky and can be formed into a smooth ball.

Put the dough into an oiled bowl then cover with plastic wrap or a damp cloth. Leave to rise for around 1½ hours.

While the dough is rising, make the filling. Put the raisins and bourbon in a small saucepan and bring to the boil, then remove from the heat and leave to infuse. Beat the butter with the maple syrup, sugar, spices and salt until you have a creamy, toffee-coloured butter.

continued...

continued…

Preheat the oven to 200°C/400°F/Gas mark 6. Line a 25–26cm/10-in round, deep cake tin with baking parchment, and butter generously. Allow the parchment to stand proud of the tin (this will help when removing the cooked buns from the tin).

Turn the risen dough out and roll or pat out into a rectangle of around 30 x 23cm/12 x 9-in. It will spring back to start with, but persevere and it will eventually yield. Spread the butter mixture over the dough, then sprinkle with the raisins, pecans and candied zest. Roll up tightly, then cut into 12 rounds.

Arrange the rounds, cut sides up/down, in the prepared cake tin. Brush with the beaten egg, then leave for around another 30 minutes and brush again. Bake in the oven for 20–25 minutes until a rich golden brown and well risen.

Meanwhile, melt the marmalade and sugar together with the bourbon or water in a small saucepan. Brush over the buns when they come out of the oven, then remove from the tin en masse by lifting out the baking parchment. Leave to cool.

An Alternative Christmas Cake

Serves 12–16

225g/1 cup butter, softened, plus extra for greasing

450g/scant 3½ cups plain (all-purpose) flour, plus extra for dusting

¾ tsp baking powder

½ tsp bicarbonate of soda

225g/1 cup plus 2 tbsp soft light brown sugar

3 large eggs

150ml/10 tbsp soured cream

Finely grated zest and juice of 1 lemon

Finely grated zest of 1 orange

Up to 75ml/5 tbsp limoncello (see page 284 for homemade) or an orange/mandarin liqueur (I favour Mandarine Napoléon)

200g/1½ cups finely diced candied lemon, citron and orange peel (see page 216 for homemade)

150g/1 cup glacé cherries or other candied fruit, chopped

For the glaze

1 tbsp limoncello or Mandarine Napoléon

200g/scant 1½ cups icing (confectioners') sugar

Boiling water

To decorate (optional)

A few rosemary sprigs

1 egg white

50g/¼ cup granulated or preserving sugar

I do love a citrus-rich fruit cake any time of year, but often around Christmas, when there is always leftover pudding lying around to nibble on, I like a lighter cake too. This still has that citrus hit, but it is cleaner-tasting than traditional Christmas cake as it doesn't contain any spice and it has a higher sponge to fruit ratio.

If you use a fairly craggy-looking Bundt tin it can be transformed into a striking snow scene that looks good displayed on the side – it also keeps quite well and, if it does go a little stale, it is dense enough to use for trifle. You can play around with the flavours here if you like, using just one kind of citrus and choosing the corresponding alcohol. It's also very good with a white chocolate icing instead of the glaze.

Preheat the oven to 170°C/340°F/Gas mark 3½. Butter and flour a deep Bundt tin. To make sure every bit of the tin is covered, including the central column, put the buttered tin in a large bag with the flour and shake it. (Alternatively, you can use a quick-release spray in place of the butter and flour.)

Put the measured flour into a bowl with the baking powder and bicarbonate of soda and whisk to combine and break up any lumps. Beat the butter and sugar together (preferably in a stand mixer or with an electric hand whisk) until light and very fluffy. Add the eggs one at a time with 2 tablespoons of the flour, folding in gently, but thoroughly, then add the rest of the flour.

Add the soured cream and zests. Measure the lemon juice and top up with enough limoncello or other citrus liqueur to give 100ml/7 tbsp liquid, then add this too. Fold this in with the candied citrus peel and glacé cherries. Scrape the mixture into the prepared tin.

continued…

continued…

Bake in the oven for around 1 hour, but start checking after 45 minutes. The cake will be done when it is springy to the touch and has slightly shrunk away from the sides. Test with a cake tester or skewer if you like – it should be batter-free if the cake is done.

Leave the cake to cool in the tin for at least 10 minutes, then turn out onto a cooling rack – it should fall straight out. Make sure the cake is completely cool before you ice it.

To make the glaze, stir the limoncello or Mandarine Napoléon into the icing (confectioners') sugar in a bowl, then carefully and gradually add just enough boiling water, starting with just a few drops, to make a consistency that is thick enough to coat the cake, rather than running right off. Drizzle the icing over the cake – covering the top and drizzling pleasingly down the sides.

Decorate as you wish – I sometimes like to use upturned rosemary sprigs, dipped in egg white and then sugar to look frosted, arranged with small figures.

Sweet Preserves And Sweets

There is one huge advantage to making citrus-based preserves: in the main, they are best made in winter. I always think this is rather a wonderful thing – creating a store of preserves to last through to the following year gives you a perfect excuse to turn your back on the grey. You can hunker down in a kitchen made warm and inviting by the preparation of colourful citrus fruit and a constantly-in-use stove. This to me is so much more in keeping with the seasons, compared with summer preserving which can seem like a chore, trapping you indoors on hot days.

Some of the recipes in this chapter are best made before Christmas, which is when you might want a store of candied citrus and homemade sweets to hand. But moving into the new year, when the bleakness of winter can feel unremitting without the distraction of Christmas to alleviate it, I can think of few things better than spending afternoons making delicious things with the new-season Seville and blood oranges, as well as preserving the last of the bergamots and mandarins.

There is no getting away from the fact that the recipes in this section rely on two old-fashioned commodities – patience and sugar. Most of the recipes aren't quick in preparation and there is some infusing to be done. However, the longest you will have to wait to eat anything once it's made is the time it takes for it to cool down.

A couple of practical points: you will need a sugar thermometer for many of the recipes you will find here. You will also need to sterilize jars. To do this, either run them through the hot cycle of a dishwasher and leave to dry, or wash in hot, soapy water, rinse and put upside down in a low oven until completely dried out. And as always, make sure you wash any fruit thoroughly before using, scrubbing as well if any are waxed.

Citrus Sugar and Syrup

These recipes are very simple and give pretty much instant results. The no-cook syrup is especially good as it is so economical – a brilliant way of extracting more flavour from your citrus discards. Do not limit yourself to sugar, by the way. You can also gently warm honey until it is just liquid, add pared zest and then decant back into the jar – this will infuse gently until the honey is used up and is particularly good over yogurt or for use in hot toddies.

Citrus Sugar

The slow method for this is simply infusing sugar with citrus peel. Use fresh or dried pieces of pared zest (see page 18) and drop it into bags or jars of sugar. Leave, shaking or turning regularly so the zest can move around. For a more subtle flavour, just use leaves when you have them.

For a fine sugar – if you use granulated sugar, you will end up with either caster (superfine) sugar or icing (confectioners') sugar depending on how long you process it – simply blitz with very fine, freshly microplaned zest or dried zest in a high-speed blender, or in batches in a coffee grinder. You can also do this with dried lemon verbena or kaffir lime leaves. Store in an airtight container, indefinitely.

Simple No-cook Syrup

This creates a very fresh-tasting syrup, useful for all kinds of things – poured over desserts, gently heated to a more liquid state and used to liven up stale cakes or sponge puddings. Just take some citrus shells that have been left over from juicing and even zesting (there is pretty much always some zest left behind, as well as some essential oils). Roughly chop up further if you like; it isn't essential. Weigh the peels and put in a bowl. Weigh out half the weight of the peels in sugar, and sprinkle this over the peels. Cover with a tea towel or similar and leave to steep for at least 3 hours, longer if you can, stirring every so often. The sugar will dissolve in this time and take on the flavour and aroma of the citrus.

Scald a piece of muslin with freshly boiled water, and use to double line a sieve or strainer. Strain the syrup, giving the peels a good squeeze as you go. Decant into sterilized bottles and store in the refrigerator.

Candied Citrus Zest

1–2 citrus fruit

100g/½ cup granulated sugar

150ml/10 tbsp water

To store

About 75g/6 tbsp granulated sugar

¼–½ tsp citric acid (optional)

Tip

The leftover syrup can also be used for syrup or sweets. Add some citrus juice and simmer for a few minutes to make a syrup for desserts and ice cream, or to pour over ice chips. And if you have a sugar thermometer, you can then use this syrup to make sweets: simply heat until it reaches 149°C/300°F, then pour onto some greased baking parchment. It will cool quickly – when it is cool enough to touch, pick it up in one large piece and work/pull it into a rope. Fold it back on itself and twist, then repeat until it feels as though it is too firm to continue without it snapping – you want to end up with a long twist around 1.5cm/½-in thick. Then cut it into sweets with scissors or a sharp knife.

This is a very quick way of preserving zest – the process is sped up because you are using just the pared zest, not the pith. It is one of those things you will not be able to stop eating – the flavour is intense and, if you add the citric acid, mouth-numbingly addictive. I use it as a garnish, or simply as a sweet (there is always a tub of these on my kitchen worktop). I will also finely chop it or blitz it to a powder to sprinkle or to give a sherbety hit.

Pare the zest from the fruit in thick strips – don't worry if a little pith is attached to the zest, this is to be expected. Slice the strips thinly, just slightly thicker than you would get if you used a parer.

Put the zest in a small saucepan and cover with cold water. Bring to the boil then immediately strain. Run under cold water, then repeat the process. Set aside the drained zest while you make the sugar syrup.

Put the sugar and water in a saucepan. Heat slowly, stirring until the sugar has completely dissolved. Add the zest and bring to the boil. Turn down and simmer gently for 10–15 minutes until the zest is translucent.

Remove the zest from the syrup with a slotted spoon and spread out on kitchen paper or a piece of baking parchment. Leave to dry for around an hour.

To store, sprinkle with sugar and keep in an airtight container. What I normally do is pound a little citric acid in a pestle and mortar until it is as powdery as icing (confectioners') sugar, and mix this with the sugar – it will make the flavours pop and will really enhance the sour qualities of the zest.

Candied Citrus Peel

4 large, 6 medium or 8 small
  citrus fruits

300g/1½ cups granulated sugar,
  plus extra for coating (optional)

300ml/1¼ cups water

When I was a child I used to plead with my mother not to put candied peel in her fruit cakes, Christmas pudding or mincemeat. I thought the taste was vile and used to spend ages picking every last bit out, as she refused to indulge me. When I started baking myself, I always left it out but soon realized it was necessary for a well-rounded flavour – however, I still couldn't bear to bite into a piece of it. What to do? Fortunately, I eventually discovered that not all candied peel came ready chopped from the supermarket and that it could be bought in large pieces – or made yourself. This was revelatory as the flavour was so different I found it quite hard to accept that they were ostensibly the same thing.

Note on making peel

There are many ways to make candied peel, and whether you leave in wedges or cut into strips is really dependent on what you want to use it for. Unless I am specifically making orangettes (or any other citrusy-ette) which are best cooked in strips, I will usually candy peel in quarters – it is easy to store that way, will keep indefinitely and can be cut to size as you need it. I add it to cakes, mincemeat, stir it through ice cream (candied lemon or orange is wonderful with a ricotta-based ice cream) or simply toss in a little sugar and eat when there is nothing else around I fancy for dessert.

My method will work well for all citrus with fairly thin or soft skin and pith. Candying citron is a more laborious process and as they are so unbelievably expensive, I think these are best bought ready candied.

Cut the fruit into quarters, vertically, then peel away the skin from the flesh – or cut it out if you prefer. You should be left with the layer of pith under the skin. If the pith is particularly thick, you can trim it down a little.

Put the peel in a bowl and cover with cold water. Soak for an hour, then drain. Transfer to a saucepan and cover again with cold water. Bring to the boil, then simmer for 5 minutes. Drain. Repeat this process twice more for lemons, limes and mandarins, three times for sweet or sour oranges and four times for grapefruit. Do not cut corners here as it is very important for making sure the peel will not be too bitter, especially if you are using white grapefruit. If you want to cut your peel into smaller strips (e.g. for orangettes) this is the time to do it.

Put the sugar and water into a saucepan. Stir over a low heat until the sugar has dissolved, then add all the peel. Simmer gently until the peel is translucent and the syrup has reduced down. At this point the thermometer should read 105–6°C/221–2°F. Transfer the peel from the saucepan using a slotted spoon and lay out on cooling racks. Either put in a very low oven (as low as it will register) with the door slightly ajar, and leave to dry out for an hour or so, or leave out overnight. Coat in sugar if you like and put in an airtight container. If kept in a cool and dark place (or in the refrigerator), it will keep indefinitely.

Candied Whole Fruit

Approx 300g/10½oz small citrus fruit

150g/¾ cup granulated sugar

100ml/⅓ cup plus 1 tbsp water

These are very similar to Greek spoon sweets, as they are kept in syrup rather than being left to dry until hard. This is best saved for small fruits – kumquats, limequats, small limes, such as Key limes, calamansi limes. It is a simple technique and you can apply it to chunks or slices of citrus fruit too if you like – I ate a bergamot version recently that was wonderful. My favourite are the limequats, and my favourite use for them is in the Chocolate Lime Puddings on page 154. You can of course slice and dice these fruits as you wish.

Put the fruit in a saucepan and cover with cold water. Bring to the boil and simmer for 5 minutes then drain. Re-cover with water and bring to the boil again. Repeat this process once more – do not skimp, as it will result in a too bitter/tough fruit.

Put the sugar in a saucepan with the water. Heat slowly, until the sugar has dissolved, then bring to the boil. Turn down and simmer gently for 10 minutes.

Take each fruit and pierce it a few times with a skewer or knife tip. Add the fruit to the syrup and simmer until tender, 15–20 minutes. Remove from the heat, cover and leave overnight.

The following day, return the saucepan to the heat and bring to the boil again. Simmer for a further 10 minutes. While still hot, decant into a warmed sterilized jar. Cool and refrigerate.

Lime and Lemon Marmalade

Makes about 4 x 450g/1lb jars

250g/9oz limes (3–4)

125g/4½oz lemons (1–2)

900ml/about 4 cups water

750g/3¾ cups granulated sugar

Note

The time your marmalade takes to reach setting point can vary depending on the levels of pectin in the fruit used. To test, chill a saucer or plate in the refrigerator, then spoon onto it a tablespoon of the boiled marmalade. Allow to cool a little, then run your finger across the surface of the marmalade. If it wrinkles then it has reached setting point; if not, then continue to boil and test again. If you have a jam or sugar thermometer, you're looking for a temperature of 105°C/221°F.

Oh, how I loved Rose's Lime Marmalade when I was a child. Decades later, I lived briefly in Dominica and discovered that for generations the island had provided Rose's with the limes they needed for their marmalade and cordial. The child me would have been round-eyed at the thought I might one day visit anywhere quite so exotic – in those days we had limes in processed foods only, and very rarely saw one fresh.

Cut all the limes and lemons in half and juice them. Put the juice in a preserving pan or large saucepan with the water. Scrape the membranes out of the citrus fruit – the easiest way to do this is to cut the halves in half again, lay them flat, and cut through the pith and peel it away.

Put the membranes and pulp in a piece of muslin or a jelly bag, secure firmly and put in the pan with the juice. Very finely slice the peel and add it to the pan. If you have time, cover and leave to stand overnight or for at least a few hours.

When you are ready to make the marmalade, put the pan on the heat and bring to the boil. Keep it covered, turn down the heat and leave to simmer for around 2 hours until the peel has softened.

Put the oven on at its lowest temperature. Put the sugar in a roasting tin and put in the oven to warm – this will help it dissolve faster, resulting in less foam and a clearer jelly.

Remove the bag of membranes and pulp from the pan, after squeezing it against the side to extract as much juice as possible. Discard. Add the warmed sugar to the pan. Cook on a low heat, stirring until it has dissolved, then turn up the heat and allow the marmalade to boil until it reaches setting point – between 7 and 10 minutes.

Remove from the heat. When the bubbling has subsided, remove any scum, then leave the marmalade to cool for around 10 minutes. Give it a good stir to evenly distribute the peel throughout the jelly, then decant into sterilized jars. Cover and leave to cool. *(Pictured opposite, left.)*

Classic Seville Orange Marmalade

Makes about 10 x 450g/1lb jars

500g/1lb 2oz Seville oranges

1.2 litres/5 cups water

Juice of 1 lemon

1kg/5 cups preserving or
    granulated sugar

Tips

If you want to pressure cook the orange peel to save time, you can do so – use half the amount of water and cook at high pressure for 10 minutes, then fast release. You should find that the peel will be perfectly soft. The resulting marmalade will not be quite as clear, but this really doesn't matter if you aren't making marmalade for competitive purposes!

It's useful to have a jar of marmalade to hand, and not just for toast and desserts. It is very good stirred into casseroles or gravy – especially with duck or pork. You can even use it in salad dressings: try whisking it into a simple olive oil and white wine vinegar vinaigrette with a tiny bit of honey and some mustard.

Seville orange marmalade is the marmalade I make without fail every year, but I do it in small batches, partly because I do like to vary texture and flavour, but also because Seville oranges are so versatile it is a shame to limit their use.

Cut the oranges in half and juice them. Scrape out all the membranes and any remaining pulp, leaving the orange shells with a clean layer of white pith still attached to the zest. Place the membranes on a large piece of muslin with any pips and tie into a bag. Put in a large bowl along with the juice.

Cut the orange skins into quarters and slice as thinly as you can – this is most easily done with a very sharp serrated knife. Add these to the bowl containing the muslin bag and juice. Add the water and leave to stand overnight.

When you are ready to make your marmalade, transfer the contents of the bowl to a preserving pan or large saucepan. Bring to the boil, then turn down to a steady simmer and cook until the orange peel is soft – this can take up to 1½ hours. When the peel is soft enough (you should be able to break a piece in two just by squeezing it lightly between your fingers) add the lemon juice and sugar.

Return to the boil and keep it at a rolling boil until setting point is reached. This will take anything from 20–30 minutes, but start testing after around 15, either by the wrinkle test (see page 220) or with a thermometer – I usually take a belts-and-braces approach and do both. When setting point has been reached, take off the heat and leave to stand for around 15 minutes, then give it a good stir to make sure the peel is evenly distributed. Transfer to sterilized jars and seal. I will usually add a few drops of Amaretto or almond extract to one or two jars, just for variety. *(Pictured on page 221, centre and right.)*

Dark and Stormy Marmalade

Makes about 10 x 450g/1lb jars

500g/1lb 2oz Seville oranges

1.2 litres/5 cups water

100g/3½oz stem ginger, rinsed and
  finely chopped

Finely grated zest and juice of 2 limes

Juice of 1 lemon

600g/3 cups preserving sugar

600g/3 cups dark muscovado sugar

30–50ml/2–3½ tbsp dark rum
  (according to taste)

A generous dash of Angostura bitters

I like to keep my regular Seville orange a pure affair, but the darker, chunkier sort lends itself well to stronger flavours. My favourite is rum and ginger and the flavour is robust enough to be reminiscent of one of my favourite cocktails, the Dark and Stormy. There is no overnight soaking in this recipe but it does require more stove time.

Put the whole oranges into a preserving pan or large saucepan and cover with the water. Bring to the boil, then turn down and simmer for up to 1½ hours, until the oranges have softened – you should be able to easily pierce the skin with the handle of a wooden spoon. Leave to cool.

When the oranges are cool enough to handle, scoop out of the water and cut in half. Scrape out the pips and the worst of the white membrane. Pile these into a square of muslin, then tie into a bundle. Return this to the pan and simmer the liquid for a further 10 minutes.

Chop the orange peel – I do this in a fairly small dice rather than strips. Add this to the pan along with the stem ginger, lime zest and juice and lemon juice. Finally, add the sugars. Stir on a low heat until the sugar has dissolved, then turn it up to a rolling boil. Check for setting point quite quickly – after 5 minutes – and at intervals.

When setting point has been reached, take off the heat and leave the marmalade to stand until it has cooled and thickened slightly. Pour in the rum and bitters, then stir once more to make sure the peel is evenly distributed. Ladle into sterilized jars and seal. *(Pictured with the Rum and Marmalade Loaf Cake, page 205.)*

Lemon Curd

Makes 1 large jar

200ml/generous ¾ cup lemon juice
(or other citrus)

Finely grated zest of 2 lemons (or
other citrus)

150g/¾ cup caster (superfine) sugar

125g/½ cup plus 1 tbsp unsalted butter

2 eggs, plus 3 egg yolks

This is the base recipe I use for most of the sourer citruses, so it will work with lemons, limes, a mixture of lemon and bergamot, sour oranges, yuzu and blood oranges – although you might want to reduce the sugar a little for the blood orange. If you expect to keep the curd for any length of time (it may last weeks in the refrigerator), make sure you have sterilized jars to decant it into. I'm sure you can think of many ways to use up a jar of curd – my favourite is to swirl it through yogurt for breakfast, or use it to fill a Victoria sponge. You could also try the Bergamot and Rose Turkish Delight Pavlova on page 166 or the Lemon Curd Slices on page 198.

Put all the ingredients into a saucepan. Cook very slowly, stirring regularly, until the sugar has dissolved and the butter has melted – it will not look pretty for a while, and may even look slightly curdled, but don't worry, it will suddenly start to homogenize.

Continue to cook on a low heat, making sure you stir constantly, otherwise any eggs in contact with the base of the pan will start to set. You will have to stir for anything from 10–20 minutes to get the right consistency – when it is ready it should thickly coat the back of your spoon and be slightly thicker than a crème anglaise. Push through a sieve into a bowl or a large sterilized jar and leave to cool – you will find it will thicken to a spreadable consistency as it does so.

Quince, Clementine and Rose Petal Jelly

Makes about 4 x 225g/½ lb jars

3 clementines (left whole)

1 large quince, roughly chopped (unpeeled and with seeds)

1 small Bramley apple

2 tbsp dried rose petals

½ cinnamon stick

Sugar (see method)

This recipe came about one Christmas. Every year I get a box of goodies from my parents in Greece that is always exciting to open – I get a thrill reminiscent of the scene in *What Katy Did At School* when they receive their Christmas boxes. The box from Greece will include quinces, clementines, pomegranates and lemons from my parents' trees, locally cured olives, olive oil, dried oregano, sage and fennel seed. On this particular year the box was delayed and some of the fruit needed using up fast – this was just one of the uses I put it to.

Put all the ingredients except the sugar into a saucepan and just cover with water. Bring to the boil and simmer until the fruits are very soft – when you can push a wooden spoon handle through the clementines without resistance it will be done, probably around an hour (alternatively, pressure cook for 10 minutes). Mash everything up a little to break up the clementines, then put into a jelly bag and strain until the pulp is quite dry – you will probably need to do this overnight.

Weigh the liquid. Put this in a preserving pan or large saucepan and add the same weight of sugar. Stir over a low heat until the sugar has dissolved, then bring to the boil and keep boiling until setting point is reached – use the wrinkle test or make sure the jelly has reached 105°C/221°F. Allow the bubbles to subside. Stir to disperse any foam – if it is proving resistant, spoon it off instead. Decant into sterilized jars, cool then seal.

Turkish Delight

Makes around 48 squares

Oil, for greasing

500g/2½ cups granulated sugar

Pared zest of 1 bergamot or lemon
(or a combination) and 1 tbsp
bergamot or lemon juice

125g/1¼ cups cornflour (cornstarch)

1 tsp cream of tartar

1 tbsp rose water

To coat

50g/heaping ⅓ cup icing
(confectioners') sugar

50g/½ cup cornflour (cornstarch)

For me, Turkish delight is a Christmas thing – growing up it could always be found next to sugared almonds, dates (the old-fashioned sort with the plastic prong for spearing) and a large bowl of whole nuts waiting to be cracked. I also remember my father producing it at key moments during a reading of *The Lion, The Witch and The Wardrobe*. There is no getting away from the fact that this recipe takes time – make it when you are happy to spend at least an hour stirring away at the stove, preferably with something good to listen to.

Lightly oil a 20cm/8-in square-sided tin. Line with plastic wrap and lightly oil again.

Put the granulated sugar into a saucepan with 600ml/ 2½ cups water and the zest. Heat slowly, stirring constantly until the sugar has dissolved, then turn up the heat and bring to the boil. Turn down slightly then leave to bubble away until you have a syrup that has reached the hard ball stage – you want it to be between 118 and 121°C/245 and 250°F. This will take around 15 minutes. Add the juice.

Meanwhile, put the cornflour (cornstarch) and cream of tartar into a saucepan with 500ml/2 cups plus 2 tbsp water, making sure you whisk out any lumps. Heat, stirring constantly, until the mixture comes to the boil. Keep stirring until it is well thickened, then remove from the heat.

Strain the sugar syrup to remove the citrus zest, then pour a small amount into the cornflour mix, whisking it in thoroughly. Gradually incorporate the rest of the sugar syrup until you have a smooth paste. Return to the heat and bring to the boil. Turn down the heat until the

continued...

mixture is very gently simmering then stir constantly and steadily for an hour, or until the mixture is very thick, and when you scrape a spoon across the bottom of the pan, it leaves a clean trail behind it.

To test whether the Turkish delight is done, take a small amount and drop it into a bowl of cold water. When it has cooled down, remove and give it a squeeze – if it is pliable but stays in a firm, unyielding lump without breaking apart, it is done. Add the rose water and stir over the heat for another minute or two until it is well combined. Immediately pour into the prepared tin, spreading it out as evenly as possible, then leave to cool.

Mix the icing (confectioners') sugar with the cornflour – this will help stop the icing sugar from melting over time. Cut the cooled Turkish delight into lumps and toss in the icing sugar mixture.

Store in a lined box that has plenty of ventilation – if you keep it anywhere airtight it will start bleeding until it all runs together in a sticky mess.

Variations

These are endless, but my favourite is lime or sour orange with orange blossom water. Simply substitute the citrus and use orange blossom water in place of the rose water. Another option is using lemon verbena leaves in place of the zest. In this instance continue to use the lemon juice.

Honey Bears

Makes about 60 small or 24 large

30g/1oz leaf gelatine

60ml/¼ cup lemon, lime, grapefruit,
sour orange or yuzu juice

50g/3 tbsp runny honey

Finely grated zest of ½ lemon or lime

A pinch each of ground ginger,
cinnamon and turmeric (optional)

Variation

If you want to use sweeter juices,
I find that sugar works better than
honey – also the flavour needs
concentrating a little. For sweet
orange, mandarin or clementine
bears, take 100ml/7 tbsp juice
and reduce it to 45ml/3 tbsp. Add
15ml/1 tbsp lemon juice and just
30g/2 tbsp sugar. Simmer together
until the sugar has melted, then
proceed as above.

These are very simple to make, especially with leaf
gelatine. You can also use powdered gelatine, but it
takes longer to dissolve and then sets far too quickly,
making it hard to get into the moulds in time. If you
want to add the merest drop of food colouring, you
can do so, but I prefer them without.

I add the spices here when I make these in winter,
especially if the kids are full of cold.

It is very easy to find the moulds for these online, and
some even come with a little pipette, which makes the
whole business much, much more straightforward.

Soak the leaf gelatine in plenty of cold water until soft.

Meanwhile, put the citrus juice, honey, zest and spices,
if using, into a saucepan and heat gently until the honey
is completely liquid. Wring out the leaf gelatine and add
to the pan. You will find it melts into the liquid very
quickly, but stir for a few moments until you are sure no
lumps remain.

Decant the liquid into a fine-lipped jug and pour the
mixture into the bear moulds – unless you have a pipette,
in which case use this instead. Leave to set. When they
are completely non-tacky, you can peel them out of their
moulds and store in an airtight container. They should
have a good bounce to them.

Chocolate Bark

Makes 1 large or 6 smaller slabs

Oil, for greasing

300g/10½oz dark, milk or white
chocolate (depending on what you
are going to add)

For the flavourings (see method)

A mixture of candied citrus peels
(see page 218 for homemade)

Stem ginger

Nuts

A few dried, crumbled rose leaves

**If I make this for home consumption, I won't bother
tempering the chocolate, as really all it does is stop
the chocolate going dull and matt when it resets.
However, this is a good recipe for presents and going
to that extra effort does improve the appearance no
end. Play around with this as much as you like – and,
if making at Christmas, a few flecks of edible gold
leaf wouldn't hurt either.**

Lightly oil a small, half-sized (about 20cm/8-in)
baking tray.

Break up the chocolate into fairly even pieces and put
200g/7oz of it into a heatproof bowl. Set the bowl over
a pan of simmering water, making sure the bowl does
not touch the water. Melt the chocolate until it is liquid,
then remove the bowl from the pan. Add the remaining
chocolate, add a sugar thermometer and stir the chocolate
until it reaches 30–32°C/86–89°F for dark or milk
chocolate or 27–28°C/80–82°F for white chocolate. At
this point your chocolate is ready to use and you will need
to act quickly.

Pour the chocolate onto the baking tray and spread it
evenly with a spatula. Sprinkle over a choice of flavours:

For dark chocolate, I like either candied orange or
grapefruit peel with finely chopped stem ginger or
chopped nuts (hazelnuts or pistachios work best).

For milk chocolate I like candied lime with salt, or
candied orange with candied fennel seeds (see opposite).

For white chocolate, try candied lemon peel, perhaps
with a few rose petals dotted about.

When the chocolate has set, break it up into pieces as
you like, or cut into bars. Store somewhere cool.

Candied Fennel Seeds

25g/2 tbsp granulated sugar

2 tbsp water

3 tbsp fennel seeds

A pinch of salt

This method works with all kinds of spices and seeds – try also caraway, aniseed, even coriander. There is also a spice I discovered recently called "cinnamon tree berry cloves", which are fabulous in chocolate, especially with lime. Candy them, then crush lightly as they are on the large side.

Put the sugar and water in a saucepan. Melt the sugar over a low heat until completely dissolved then turn up the heat and boil for 2–3 minutes until the mixture has bubbled up and turned syrupy. Add the fennel seeds and salt. Stir until the mixture suddenly turns from sticky to powdery. As soon as this has happened, remove from the heat and stir until all the seeds are completely separate from one another and coated in a powdered sugar. These are very versatile on their own, but you can also add dried citrus to them if you like – try blitzed lemon zest.

Chewy Citrus Caramels

Makes about 64

100g/7 tbsp butter, plus extra, softened, for greasing

300ml/1¼ cups double (heavy) cream

Strips of pared zest from 1 large or 2 small citrus fruits

½ vanilla pod

A piece of cinnamon stick (optional)

A few allspice berries, lightly crushed (optional)

A few cardamom pods (optional)

A pinch of salt

200g/1 cup granulated sugar

150g/7 tbsp golden syrup

50ml/3½ tbsp water

These are based on one of my favourite things – the pralines you get in the US that are soft and creamy, quite unlike the hard, jaw-sealing toffee we are used to in the UK. You can add any citrus flavour to these – I favour grapefruit, mandarin or lemon zest as perfect foils for all the cream and butter. Either go for a clean flavour here or add spices – those listed are just suggestions; try herbs or other spices. You can also add a little alcohol towards the end – rum is particularly good.

Butter a square 20cm/8-in baking tin and line with plastic wrap, making sure it overlaps the sides so the caramel will be easy to remove.

Put the cream in a saucepan with the zest, vanilla and any other aromatic you are using, if any. Heat gently until just below boiling point, then remove from the heat and leave to infuse until quite cool. If you can, leave for an hour or so, or even overnight.

Reheat the cream, this time with the butter and salt added to it. When the butter has melted, remove from the heat and strain into a jug.

Put the sugar and golden syrup in a saucepan with the water. Do not stir. Leave on a medium to high heat until it has melted into a light golden syrup. When it starts to boil rapidly, add your sugar thermometer – it will not take long to get up to 127°C/260°F and should turn very slightly darker.

Remove from the heat. Gradually pour the cream mixture into the sugar mixture, whisking constantly. Return the saucepan to a medium–high heat and bring back to the

continued…

boil, again without stirring. It will foam up and will look somewhere between a frothy banana or butterscotch milkshake. Continue to heat, stirring regularly with a rubber spatula, until the thermometer reads around 130–133°C/266–271°F; this will take a few minutes. When it reaches this temperature, remove from the heat and start whisking with a balloon whisk – keep whisking until the caramel is very smooth and all the bubbles have subsided. Pour into the prepared tin – it will be liquid enough to form a smooth, even layer. Drop it a couple of times onto the work surface just to remove any air bubbles.

Leave to set for several hours or overnight, then cut into squares with a sharp knife, either sprayed with quick-release spray or heated up under a flame. Wrap each in wax paper and twist. How many you get depends on size – I normally cut it into 8 x 8, giving 64 pieces.

Note

To make a caramel sauce instead of a chewy caramel, proceed as above, but increase the amount of cream to 500ml/2 cups plus 1 tbsp, then instead of heating the sugar and cream mixture to any particular temperature, just warm gently until smooth. You can store this in the refrigerator, reheating when needed – it is very good poured over ice cream.

Citrus-Flecked Lollies with Sherbet

Makes about 24

300g/1½ cups granulated sugar

Grated zest of 1 large or 2 small citrus

150g/7 tbsp golden syrup

½ tsp cream of tartar

200ml/¾ cup plus 1 tbsp water

For the sherbet

Candied citrus zest (see page 216)

The easiest way to make these is with a lolly mould, but there is nothing wrong with doing them free form (as shown) – non-uniformity has a certain charm. You will need lolly sticks, however.

Blitz 50g/¼ cup of the sugar with the citrus zest in a small food processor – this will give a good uniformity of flavour to the lollies. Put the blitzed sugar and zest, the remaining sugar and the golden syrup in a small saucepan. Add the cream of tartar and water.

Warm gently, stirring constantly, until the sugar and syrup have melted, then turn up the heat and bring to the boil. Keep it going until the syrup reaches 154°C/309°F, then remove from the heat.

Divide the syrup between the lolly moulds and add the lolly sticks. If you don't have lolly moulds, dollop spoonfuls onto greased baking parchment, making sure you leave enough space to place a lolly stick (see picture opposite) on each one. Leave the lollies to cool completely before removing them from the moulds or baking parchment.

For the sherbet, simply take a quantity of candied citrus zest along with the sugar and citric acid it is stored with. Make sure it is completely dry, then blitz to a fine powder in a small food processor. Taste, and add a little more citric acid or sugar as you think necessary.

Drinks

It is hard to put into words the influence citrus fruits have had and continue to have on the things we drink. They can be found in just about everything, except perhaps in builder's tea and in coffee, and even there they have made inroads. How many people start the day with a slice of lemon floating in a cup of water? And how many others take the same lemon slice or twist for granted in the first drink of the evening? We scent tea with bergamot and other citrusy aromatics, and drink them with a slice of lemon too. We make iced tea with lemon, herbal teas with orange blossom, lime leaves, verbena and lemongrass, we use citrus to make flavours such as elderflower sing in cordials, as well as giving them starring roles in presses and all manner of cooling lemonades. Citrus and alcohol combinations range from the sweet, sour, fizzy mixes from the Americas to the very grown-up herbal and bitter notes found in orange-infused spirits and liqueurs popular in Europe. They are essential in all kinds of cocktails and punches as well as wine-based drinks such as sangria. We use them medicinally in hot toddies and barley waters. What on earth did we do without them?

Cold Infusions and Iced Teas

A cold infusion of tea has one main advantage over traditionally made iced tea – and that is that there isn't really any need for added sugar as the flavour is pretty much tannin free, making it purer, cleaner, sweeter. However, it does need a long infusion – usually around 10–12 hours of steeping in the refrigerator.

To make, take a 1-litre/4-cup bottle that you can store in the door of your refrigerator. Add a teaspoon of any loose tea you like then add any aromatics. Fill the bottle with filtered water, then put into the refrigerator to infuse. Taste at intervals until it has reached the strength you like, then strain and store. Or you can just leave everything in and keep letting it get stronger. My favourite combinations are:

White tea, with a teaspoon of orange blossom and pared lime zest

White tea with rose petals and pared lemon zest

Jasmine tea with a kaffir lime leaf and pared lime zest

Green tea with pared grapefruit zest

Russian Caravan (or something with similar smoky flavours) with pared mandarin and orange zest

Peppermint tea with lime zest and, on serving, slices of cucumber

You can also cold-brew coffee, which is actually my favourite way to drink it – again, because it is less acidic on the stomach and I find the flavours much more distinct, and coffee and citrus go surprisingly well together – see Orange and Coffee Liqueur on page 250. It is almost as easy as the tea – simply make sure you have coarsely ground coffee beans (the texture of breadcrumbs), put in the bottom of a cafetière, or a large bottle. The strength is up to you, but I use around 1 tablespoon per 240ml/1 cup. Leave to stand for around 12 hours, then either press or strain. To add citrus notes, you can add pared zest along with the coffee, but really just serving over ice with lots of slices of lemon and lime makes for a very refreshing drink. My husband likes adding a sliver of chilli to the coffee while it is brewing too.

Proper Lemon Iced Tea

This is an absolute classic. I don't mess around with it too much, but you can experiment with similar flavour combinations listed for the cold-infused tea (see page 237). You can use loose leaf tea or bags for this. Take 2 tea bags or 2 teaspoons of loose leaf tea along with the freshly pared zest of a lemon, then pour over 1 litre/generous 4 cups freshly boiled water. Add ginger or mint as well if you like. Leave to infuse for 2–3 minutes or until it is a little stronger than you would normally brew it (this because it will be diluted). Strain then add the juice of a lemon. Taste and start adding sugar or honey to sweeten – again, you will need a little more than you think, because it will taste sweeter while still hot or warm. Leave until it is completely cool, then serve over ice with lots more mint leaves and slices of lemon. I love making this with a pinch of a smoky-flavoured tea as well – an oolong or lapsang souchong.

Hot Toddy

I am sure I am not the only one who has strong opinions on the contents of a hot toddy. I have been making these for as long as I can remember. When young, I think I was probably allowed a teaspoon of alcohol in my honey and lemon – now I glug it in with abandon. I prefer rum to anything else, but I know plenty who can't imagine it made with anything other than whisky. Each to their own.

You can also make a toddy with marmalade or jam. I particularly like a yuzu honey jam called Yujacha which Koreans swear by as a soothing, cold-busting remedy. Simply add a couple of teaspoons to a mug of hot water, alcohol strictly optional.

Classic Hot Toddy

1 pared piece of lemon zest and juice of 1 lemon

2 heaped tsp runny honey

A measure or two of whisky, rum or brandy

Optional Extras

Juice of 1 orange (for more vitamin C)

A couple of cloves, a piece of cinnamon stick and
  a pinch of turmeric (for something slightly more ayurvedic)

This is simplicity itself. Put all the ingredients into a mug and top with freshly boiled water. Stir until the honey has dissolved, then drink.

A Few Favourite Hot Teas

For years I have been trying to wean myself off my builder's tea habit, but it wasn't until I started experimenting with citrus and tea that I managed to limit it. The classic of course is highly perfumed Earl Grey with a slice of lemon – I like this with a slice of orange instead – but you can create any combination you like at home if you have a selection of different teas and some dried aromatics. Add dried citrus peel, fresh leaves or blossoms to your tea, either by putting it in the same caddy as the tea to infuse, or adding it at the same time as the water.

Moroccan Mint and Lemon Verbena Tea

There are lots of types of Moroccan tea – it isn't all about mint. However, I really like the combination of mint and lemon verbena and so use both here.

Pour some boiling water into a teapot and swirl it round just to warm. Pour out. Put a teaspoon of green tea in the teapot with a few fresh mint leaves and a few fresh or dried lemon verbena leaves and add just-boiled water. Leave to steep for a few minutes, then serve with honey or sugar cubes to sweeten.

Black Tea with Orange Blossom and Orange

This tea is served up in Sally Butcher's Peckham café and Aladdin's cave, Persepolis. For each person, use a teaspoon of black tea and add a teaspoon of dried orange blossoms. Steep until the tea is the strength you like. Serve with a slice of orange, another pinch of orange blossom and honey to taste.

This is also lovely cold-brewed and is very refreshing on a hot day. Put a teaspoon of black or white tea in a bottle with a piece of dried orange zest and a teaspoon of orange blossom flowers. Leave for several hours or overnight then strain and serve in glasses over ice.

Bush Tea

This is a tea we used to make as a bedtime digestive when I lived in the Caribbean. It's made with lemongrass, or citronella as it is called by the locals. Simply steep muddled lemongrass and lime leaves in freshly boiled water. In winter I will add a pinch of turmeric to this, as well as a sliver of cinnamon stick and a couple of allspice berries. Warming.

Cordials

Look at recipes for a whole variety of cordials and you will find few that don't contain citrus of some sort. As much as I love these (elderflower and lemon, or blackberry and lime in particular are both wonderful), here I have chosen three favourites in which citrus is the dominant flavour. The mandarin cordial works well as a blueprint – exchange the mandarins and limes for blood oranges, for example.

Makes about 700ml/1¼ pints

Grated zest and juice of 6 mandarins

Grated zest and juice of 2 limes

1 tsp black peppercorns, lightly crushed

Stems from a bunch of basil, finely chopped

350ml/1½ cups water

300ml/1½ cups granulated sugar (white gives a purer colour)

Mandarin, Lime and Basil Cordial

Measure the mandarin and lime juices – they should come to around 240ml/1 cup. Put the zests, juice and black peppercorns into a sterilized heatproof bowl or jug. Put the basil stems in a saucepan and pour over the water and sugar. Heat slowly until the sugar has completely dissolved. Bring to the boil then simmer for 5 minutes.

Pour the hot syrup over the contents of the bowl. Cover the bowl with plastic wrap, then leave to stand for at least 12 hours.

Scald some muslin and use it to double line a sieve or colander. Strain the syrup into a jug, then pour it into sterilized bottles. Seal and store somewhere cool. Once you have opened it, it is best kept in the refrigerator.

Cocktail suggestion

I don't think you can improve on simply mixing this with prosecco. However, you could make a rum-based drink, similar to a mojito, using this cordial in place of sugar.

Makes about 500ml/1 pint

Grated zest and juice of 1 grapefruit
(around 150ml/⅔ cup juice)

A few thin slices of Scotch bonnet chilli
(more if using a milder variety
of chilli)

A few allspice berries, lightly crushed

350ml/1½ cups water

150g/¾ cup granulated sugar

Grapefruit, Allspice and Chilli Cordial

Put the zest, juice, chilli and allspice berries in a sterilized
heatproof bowl or jug. Put the water and sugar in a
saucepan and heat slowly until the sugar has completely
dissolved. Bring to the boil then simmer for 5 minutes.

Pour the sugar syrup over the ingredients in the bowl
and continue as for Mandarin, Lime and Basil Cordial
(see opposite).

Cocktail suggestion

Try adding a couple of tablespoons of this to a
measure of gin. Muddle in a couple of mint leaves and
a couple of twists of grapefruit, then top with plenty of
ice and tonic water.

Makes about 700ml/1½ pints

A handful of kaffir lime leaves, lightly
bruised or shredded

Grated zest and juice of 2 limes

Grated zest and juice of 2 lemons

3–4 lemongrass stalks, bruised with the
back of a knife

500ml/2 cups plus 2 tbsp water

300g/1½ cups granulated sugar

Kaffir Lime Leaf with Lime and Lemongrass Cordial

Put the lime leaves, zests, juices and lemongrass into a
large sterilized heatproof bowl and add the discarded
citrus shells too. Put the water and sugar in a saucepan
and heat slowly until the sugar has completely dissolved.
Bring to the boil then simmer for 5 minutes.

Pour the sugar syrup over the ingredients in the bowl
and continue as for Mandarin, Lime and Basil Cordial
(see opposite).

Cocktail suggestion

Take 2 tablespoons cordial and add either 1 tablespoon
crème de mûre or muddle in a handful of ripe blackberries.
Add a shot of vodka and top with prosecco or sparkling
water: two very different drinks, both excellent.

Classic Barley Water

Makes about 500ml/1 pint

50g/generous ¼ cup pearl barley
  (barley)

Pared zest of 1 lemon or orange

500ml/generous 2 cups boiling water

1 tbsp runny honey or sugar

For years lemon or orange barley made me think of a very particular brand of cordial, purely because of its long-standing association with Wimbledon's ball boys. However, barley water is good when made at home. It's useful for anyone – child or adult – who needs very gentle nutrition.

Wash the barley, then put in a saucepan with the pared zest. Cover with cold water, bring to the boil and boil for 3 minutes – this will help remove any bitterness from both the barley and the zest. Strain and put the barley and zest into a jug. Cover with the boiling water, then stir in the honey or sugar until dissolved. Leave to infuse until the water has cooled down, then strain, discarding the barley and zest. Keep in the refrigerator.

Punch – the long and the short of it

Serves 8

100ml/7 tbsp lime juice

200ml/generous ¾ cup sugar syrup
(100ml/7 tbsp granulated sugar
dissolved in 100ml/7 tbsp
boiling water)

300ml/1¼ cups white or golden rum
(not a dark one; you want caramel,
not molasses)

200ml/generous ¾ cup sour orange
juice mixed with 200ml/generous
¾ cup water or sweet orange juice

To serve

Ice

Slices of limes

A dash of grenadine

A generous dash of Angostura bitters

A rasp of nutmeg

Wherever you find limes growing abundantly, you will find drinks that happily couple them with the local spirit. The shorter versions of these follow the same pattern – lime and sugar or sugar syrup are muddled together, perhaps with another aromatic such as mint, before the spirit is added. In the Caribbean, we have the Ti'Punch, found in the French islands, made with the local rhum agricole. In Brazil cachaça mixes with muddled limes and mint for caipirinha; in Peru, the same drink is made with pisco. A slightly longer drink is the rum-based mojito or the tequila-based margarita, but for me, these are still on the short side. I have spent many evenings when all of these are made one after another, and as much as I love them, it is an exhausting pastime. I would much rather make a long drink which does not need replenishing every 5 minutes.

So then to my favourite rum punch… I strongly believe the best rum punches in the world are to be found on the Caribbean island of Nevis. I was once given a freshly made bottle as a welcome gift and spent weeks trying to reverse engineer it – my only clue was sour oranges. I do now think this recipe nails it. It follows the classic "1 of sour, 2 of sweet, 3 of strong and 4 of weak". Stick to this and you can't go too far wrong. Mine is just made more sour by the weak including sour as well as sweet orange. This makes quite a large amount, but it seems to disappear quickly and you can cut it down considerably if you wish.

Mix together the lime juice, sugar syrup, rum and sour orange juice and water mixture. Chill well. Fill highball glasses with ice and lime slices, then pour over the punch mixture. Add a dash of grenadine and Angostura bitters, then grate over a little nutmeg.

Lemonade

Makes about 1 litre/2 pints

4 lemons (or 6 limes, or 3 lemons and 2 limes)

100–150g/½–¾ cup caster (superfine) sugar, to taste

1 litre/scant 4 cups water, or a mixture of water and sparkling water

This recipe works just as well with limes or with a combination of lemons and limes, as limes add a sherbety element to the flavour. This is a quick version as no steeping is necessary. It is lovely garnished with citrus slices, cucumber slices, mint leaves and borage flowers, and is also good with a slug of vodka, gin, or if using limes, rum.

Roughly chop the half the citrus and put in a food processor. Finely grate the zest and squeeze the juice of the remaining fruit. Add to the food processor with the sugar (go for the lower quantity if you prefer it sharp, more if you have a sweet tooth) and 240ml/1 cup of the water and blitz until everything is finely chopped. You should find the sugar has dissolved.

Strain through a sieve into a large jug with plenty of ice, and top with the remaining water or sparkling water. Add more sugar to taste, if needed.

Variations

Preserved Lemonade

This is unbelievably refreshing. It is based on a Vietnamese recipe, and you can use any citrus which has been preserved the traditional way – I really love limequats for this, but lemons, limes and sour oranges are all good. It is very simple. Put ¼–½ preserved lemon or similar in a glass along with some granulated sugar – start with a couple of teaspoons. Muddle it all together to release the juices from the citrus, then top with sparkling water. Taste and adjust the sweetness levels if necessary. Try adding cucumber slices for sharp contrast or add a measure of rum or vodka for something alcoholic.

The Quickest Version

This is a very quick and easy drink, found wherever you get fresh limes. Simply take the juice of 2 limes, mix with ½ tsp sugar, slightly more of salt and top with sparkling water. I like to add a dash of bitters as well. I am told it makes a very good hangover cure – as a friend of mine says: "Like your own electrolyte sachet but nicer."

Liqueurs and Cellos

Makes about 1 litre/2 pints

7 citrus fruit (I recommend lemon, blood or sour orange, bergamot, mandarin, yuzu; you need 1 fruit for every 75ml/5 tbsp alcohol, 2 if they are particularly small)

500ml/2 cups plus 2 tbsp vodka or white rum

400g/2 cups granulated sugar

400ml/scant 1¾ cups filtered water (for clarity)

I started experimenting with different types of cellos in the run-up to Christmas one year, which was well timed as some of them made wonderful Christmas drinks as well as pretty decent presents. I found it best to start with very small batches (using around 300ml/1¼ cups alcohol) – I think this is the way to go until you decide which of them you really love. My absolute favourite turned out to be bergamot, which I drank all over Christmas mixed with prosecco. I found I wasn't very keen on the kaffir lime, which I believe belongs firmly in the "savoury" section, with only very occasional forays into the sweet. Thanks to the generosity of a globe-trotting friend, I was able to make a yuzucello, which was spectacular. Do try it if you ever get the chance.

This is a very simple recipe, although it does require a certain amount of tasting towards the end. The quantities can easily be halved if you want to experiment with different flavours. I can't give you an exact amount this recipe will make as it does depend on how much sugar syrup you add, but it will make up to 1 litre/2 pints.

Zest the fruit, either with a microplane or in strips with a swivel peeler. Put in a sealed glass container with the vodka or rum. Leave to infuse at room temperature for several days, or up to 3 weeks. The rule of thumb is that no more flavour is to be had once the zest has turned white, but this isn't exact. I find 5–7 days will give quite a pronounced flavour, making this a very useful recipe if you want fast results.

Make a sugar syrup. Put the sugar and water in a saucepan. Heat gently, stirring constantly until the sugar has dissolved, then leave to simmer for 15 minutes. Remove from the heat and cool.

Start mixing the sugar syrup and infused alcohol. I start with the same amount of syrup to alcohol, mixing thoroughly and tasting. Add more sugar syrup until you are happy with the flavour – the more you add, the smoother and sweeter your cello will become.

Decant into a jug and pour into sterilized bottles.

Vin de Pamplemousse

Makes about 1.5 litres/3 pints

Peel of 3 pink or ruby grapefruit
Peel of 1 lemon
½ vanilla pod
¼ cinnamon stick
1 litre/generous 4 cups rosé wine
200ml/about ¾ cup vodka
50ml/3½ tbsp rum
200g/1 cup granulated sugar

My friend Fi makes the best vin d'orange, which is lovely but has already appeared in print, and I felt the need to experiment. So I have used her blueprint and made instead a grapefruit version which really is quite stunning.

Preheat your oven to 150°C/300°F/Gas mark 2. Put the grapefruit and lemon peel on a baking sheet and put in the oven for around 45 minutes to an hour until it is dry, aromatic and just starting to brown.

Put the peel into a large sterilized jar or wide-lipped bottle with the pieces of vanilla pod and cinnamon stick. Add the remaining ingredients, then seal, making sure it is airtight. Leave somewhere cool and dark for 4–6 weeks, turning regularly to ensure the sugar dissolves properly. Start tasting after 4 weeks. When you are happy that the grapefruit flavour shines through, strain the liquid through blanched muslin or a coffee filter into sterilized bottles. Once opened, keep refrigerated.

Orange and Coffee Liqueur

Makes about 1 litre/2 pints

2 Seville oranges

44 (6g/1 heaped tbsp) medium roast
coffee beans

44 tsp (250g/2¼ cups) sugar

1 litre/generous 4 cups golden rum

I am not usually a fan of oranges and alcohol – I am not keen on any of the orange-based liqueurs and consider negroni and other orange-heavy cocktails involving gin the devil's work. However, this is something else entirely – it is based on a recipe called The 44 Cordial, as it requires 44 coffee beans, 44 sugar cubes and is steeped for 44 days. I have given measurements in weight as well to avoid laborious counting on your part.

This is normally made with a large navel orange, but sour oranges are prevalent all over the Caribbean and have – in my opinion – a much more fragrant oil. They are also the type of orange normally used in orange liqueurs. So I make this when Seville oranges are in season. This is also normally made with white rum – again, I prefer a golden one for slightly more depth and caramel notes. Use a half decent one if you can; you won't regret it.

Wash and dry the oranges thoroughly. Cut slits evenly all over the orange skin and push the coffee beans in. Put in a large preserving jar and cover with the sugar. Pour over the rum and seal.

Leave to steep for 44 days (6 weeks) then strain into clean, sterilized bottles. Do not leave this for longer as I did the first time I made it – the bitter notes will become too dominant.

Cocktail suggestion

This is a good sipping drink, but I also like making an orange version of a "Black Lemon" – so the "Black Orange", if you will – a take on the vodka martini. Simply take 1 shot of this liqueur, 1 shot of espresso and 2 shots of frozen vodka. Shake over ice then strain into a frozen glass and garnish with a twist of pared orange.

Index

Index

253

Index

Acknowledgements

A trio of brilliant people helped to get this book off the ground. Ed Griffiths helped me to realise that my love of citrus would translate well into a book – and gave me some very good advice along the way, particularly on Japanese food. Clare Hulton, my wonderful agent, believed in the book, as did my equally wonderful editor, Sarah Lavelle. Thank you all and extra thanks to Sarah for being so patient with me during the writing process.

Thanks to the supremely talented team on the photoshoot: Mowie Kay, Iris Bromet, Laurie Perry, Katie Marshall and especially Marina Filippelli. I couldn't be happier with the results.

Thank you to everyone at Quadrille, especially Nicola Ellis for the beautiful design and stunning cover. Thank you also to Sally Somers for making the copy-editing process so painless.

So many fellow food writers, friends and family helped me during the writing of this book. Xanthe Clay sent me kaffir limes, finger limes and even yuzu from Japan. Sally Butcher and her husband Jamshid were incredibly hospitable and helpful on the role of citrus in the Middle East. Kerstin Rogers sent me numerous citrus-related links, Tim Hayward gave advice on citrus and knives and Charlie Hicks helped me on availability and seasonality. Both Fiona Kirkpatrick and Alanna Lauder gave me tips on citrus drinks. Naomi Hourihane came to my rescue with rosemary flowers. Jinny Johnson was always at the other end of the phone, giving advice but often just letting me think out loud.

Special thanks to my mother, who taught me to cook from first principles and who during the course of this book, brainstormed with me, searched out old recipes and sent me ingredients to play with, including citrus leaves from her trees in Greece.

Finally, as always, thanks to Shariq, Lilly and Adam, who get better at constructive criticism with every book I write and who are a pleasure to cook for. Stellar testers, all.